To New Rochelle Public Library

With compliments,

Muita C. Wang

The Essentials of Chinese Thought:
Past and Present

# The Essentials of Chinese Thought:
## Past and Present

*Minta C. Wang*

620751

**ABOUT FACE PRESS
WESTBURY, NEW YORK**

ISBN 0-914551-00-0

*In memory of my mother*

# Contents

Preface    9

1.   The Earliest Times    11

2.   Confucius    18

3.   Mo Tzu    29

4.   The Taoists: Lao Tzu and Chuang Tzu    35

5.   Prominent Followers of Confucius: Mencius and Hsün Tzu    41

6.   The Legalists: Shang Yang, Han Fei, and Li Ssu    47

7.   Philosophical Synthesis of the Han    54

8.   Neo-Taoism and Buddhism    61

9.   Neo-Confucianism and the Reaction against Neo-Confucianism    72

10.   Sun Yat-sen    81

11.   Leading Proponents of a New Culture: Ch'en Tu-hsiu and Hu Shih    93

12.   Mao Tse-tung    104

13.   Conclusion    127

Bibliography    133

Index    144

# Preface

*T*his introductory work surveys the essentials of Chinese thought from ancient times to the present. Written in the context of Chinese history, it covers only the leading schools of Chinese philosophy, i.e., schools of thought or individuals which have had long lasting influence on the Chinese mind or strong influence during a certain period of time. It also covers some philosophies in whole or in part borrowed from the thought of other peoples, such as Buddhism, Pragmatism, and Marxism. It is intended for use in any basic course on Chinese history and culture; it will serve also as an introduction to the subject for those with little knowledge of China or the Chinese language.

It is presented as concisely and in as simple language as possible, yet any reader who is interested in a more in-depth study will find guidance in the notes and in the bibliography at the end of the book.

In writing this manuscript and revising it I owe thanks to a number of friends. I am in debt to Dr. Richard D. Breslin, Vice President for Academic Affairs of Iona College, who initiated the Faculty Enrichment Program under which I was granted a one-course remission for two consecutive semesters to speed up my writing of this manuscript. I am deeply grateful to Professor Joseph G.E. Hopkins for his valuable advice and encouragement.

To my brother Ling my great appreciation for the book jacket which he designed for me. To my sister Nora my gratitude for some of the reference material which she bought me as a gift.

Finally, to my husband Ernest who is forever patient and tolerant, I owe more than I can express.

# 1

# The Earliest Times

*T*he Chinese people generally believe that their history and culture are about five thousand years old. Legend[1] has it that during the first half of the third millennium B.C. there lived a number of culture-heroes who possessed superhuman goodness and wisdom. They brought to the people various arts of civilization and as a result, were made rulers by the people. Among them were Yu-ch'ao who taught the people how to build shelters with wood; Sui-jen who showed them how to bore wood and get fire; and Fu-hsi who established the order for man and woman to marry and live together as husband and wife. He also invented writing, devised a calendar, and discovered the eight trigrams for divination.[2] Ruler Shen-nung introduced various tools for farming. Ruler Huang-ti, known to the West as the Yellow Emperor, introduced governmental institutions. It was he who finally defeated the invaders and cleared North China for Chinese settlement.

During the second half of the third millennium B.C. there were Yao and Shun, known as sage-kings because of their virtue and wisdom. They, like Plato's philosopher-kings, ruled entirely for the well-being of the people. It has been said that King Yao, instead of following the rule of hereditary succession, passed over his incompetent son to select Shun as his successor. King Shun divided the domain into twelve provinces, standardized weights and measures, and established a distinguished administration. King Yü, also known as a sage-king, was the founder of the Hsia dynasty (ca. 1994-1523 B.C.).[3] He spent thirteen years in his endeavor to regulate rivers and watercourses in order to prevent the floods that had frequently caused damage to the people.

The last ruler of the Hsia dynasty was cruel to the people. He was overthrown by King T'ang, the sage-king who founded the Shang (also known as Yin) dynasty (ca. 1523-1028 B.C.). Most modern historians agree that Shang represents the beginning of the Chinese historic period.[4]

The last ruler of the Shang dynasty was again tyrannical. Rebellion led to his overthrow and the replacement of his dynasty with that of Chou. Chou, founded by King Wen and his son King Wu, both sage-kings, was a long dynasty (ca. 1027-256 B.C.). It is sometimes divided into three periods: Early Chou (ca. 1027-771 B.C.) when the kings of hereditary succession actually governed their vassals, who were the lords of the various feudal states of the kingdom; Middle Chou (ca. 771-473 B.C.) when the power of the kings gradually passed into the hands of a few strong lords of feudal states; and Late Chou (ca. 473-256 B.C.) when the struggle for hegemony over the kingdom narrowed to a contest between the lords of two feudal states, Ch'in and Ch'u.[5]

It was during the period of Middle Chou that Confucius (ca. 551-479 B.C.) lived. Most modern historians regard him as the first Chinese who developed a true system of thought.[6]

Certain Chinese concepts, however, had existed before the time of Confucius. They could be traced in the Five Classics and their commentaries[7] and in the inscriptions on ancient objects discovered through archeological excavation. Some of these concepts—religious, political, and social—may be presented as follows.

Before the periods of Hsia and Shang, the Chinese people, like the ancient Greeks, believed in many nature gods—gods of the objects and the phenomena of nature, such as the gods of the sun, moon, stars, mountains, and rivers; of the wind, rain, and thunder. They also believed in the existence of the spirits of their ancestors following death. Their rulers made sacrifices to these deities in order to secure divine favors and protection.

With the coming of the Hsia and Shang dynasties the

concept of the existence of a Supreme Being arose. During the Shang, this supreme being was sometimes referred to as T'ien or "Heaven" and at other times, as Shang-ti or "Lord-on-High." He was regarded as the supreme anthropomorphic deity of the universe[8] and he presided over an elaborate hierarchy of lesser deities who paid him allegiance. He was the divine ruler who regulated the working of the universe on the one hand and who exerted strong influence on human society on the other. He sent blessings or calamities and approved or disapproved human undertakings of all kinds. The lesser deities—the nature gods and the spirits of ancestors—were also believed to exert some definite influence upon human affairs. Therefore, sacrifices to Heaven and other deities were made regularly by the rulers of the people. Great care was taken so that each deity would be served with sacrifice to his preference. The intention was still one of pleasing the powerful deities in order to secure blessings from them or avoid calamities. Throughout Early Chou this basic religious concept persisted.

As early as the time of the Hsia dynasty it was believed that the king should be a good example to his government officials and other subordinates. He should lead the way in the proper performance of the duties of government, because the work was Heaven's and men were to act for Heaven.

"Mandate of Heaven" was the ancient Chinese political concept that prevailed during Early Chou. It was claimed that the ruler of the people was appointed by Heaven. So long as his heirs carried out their religious and administrative duties properly, they would be entitled to rule. Should any heir be degenerate or cruel to the people, he would be abandoned by Heaven and would be replaced with a new man and a new dynasty worthy of the mandate. Because the last ruler of the Hsia dynasty was evil, Heaven discarded him, appointed King T'ang to replace him, and established the Shang dynasty. Likewise, the last ruler of the Shang dynasty was evil, so he lost the mandate of Heaven to King Wen and King Wu of the Chou dynasty. As noted by Professor Creel, this concept established "in theory, the principle that the rulers existed for the sake of the people, rather than the reverse. . . ."[9] It was used to justify the overthrow and replacement of one dynasty by another, and helped temper the traditional absolutism of the ruler. In order not to lose the mandate of Heaven the ruler had to make an effort to carry out his duties properly.

As is reflected in the *Book of Poetry*, the people of Early Chou were permitted to satirize idle and greedy government officials and complain against their oppression and extortion. They could even openly express their desire to leave the country for a better land.[10]

In the society of ancient China the orderly family was considered important. For a family to be orderly each of its members had to carry out his respective moral obligations. Filial piety or loving care for one's parents and tender regard for one's younger brothers were emphasized. On the other hand, love for one's sons and respect for one's elder brothers were expected in return. During Early Chou, failure to carry out one's family obligations was regarded as not only a moral but also a legal offense and was punishable under penal law.[11]

The people of ancient China believed that man was mortal but that his virtues, achievements, and words were immortal. The best course for a man was to establish himself as virtuous; the next best, to achieve something; after that to utter memorable words. Each of these—his virtue, his achievement, and his words—would bear its influence beyond his lifetime, and in that sense he would be immortal.[12]

**Notes**

1. There are different versions of the legend. One version goes back to time immemorial, when P'an-ku, ancestor of Chinese ancestors, emerged and made the heaven and earth. The myth of P'an-ku, however, cannot be compared with the creation story of the Bible. The Chinese people have never attached much importance to P'an-ku or to when and how the universe was created. Instead, they lay emphasis on their culture-heroes and sage-kings.

2. The eight trigrams are all the possible permutations of three-line combinations of complete or broken lines or both. They are as follows:

☰ ☱ ☲ ☳ ☴ ☵ ☶ ☷

It is not clear how they were used to foretell events but is said that they later served as the basis of the 64 hexagrams of the *Book of Changes*.

It is also not clear how divination was practiced at this time, although it is known that at some time before and during the Shang dynasty (ca. 1523-1028

B.C.) bones of cattle or tortoise shells were used for divination. A small groove was carved on one side of the bone or the under-shell of a tortoise. Heat was then applied near the groove, producing cracks that would be read and interpreted by the diviner. Presumably, one of the methods of interpretation was to compare the line formation of the cracks to the trigram that it resembled most. See Note 7 on the *Book of Changes* for further explanation.

3. These and later dates have been adopted from the Chronological Table of Professor L. C. Goodrich, *A Short History of the Chinese People,* 4th ed. (New York: Harper & Row, 1969), pp. 261-62.

4. Since no ancient Chinese writing system has been identified with a period earlier than the Shang dynasty, Shang is taken as the beginning of the Chinese historic period. On the other hand, the Shang writing system was so well-developed that it could have existed in a simpler form during an earlier period.

The kings of the second half of the third millennium B.C. and those of the Hsia dynasty cannot very well be called legendary, since records about them as well as later kings of the historical periods appear in the *Book of History.*

5. See Note ten, ch. 1 of L. C. Goodrich, *A Short History of the Chinese People,* p. 18.

6. Yu-lan Fung, *A History of Chinese Philosophy,* vol. 1 (Derk Bodde, trans.) (Princeton, New Jersey: Princeton University Press, 1952), p. 8.

7. The Five Classics, upheld by all Confucians, are sometimes known to the West as Confucian Classics. They cover the I Ching or *Book of Changes,* the Shu Ching or *Book of History* (also translated as the *Book of Historical Documents),* the Shih Ching or *Book of Poetry* (also translated as the *Book of Odes* or the *Book of Songs),* the *Ritual,* the important part of which is known as the *Li Chi* or *Book of Rites,* and the Ch'un-Ch-iu or *Spring and Autumn Annals.*

The *Book of Changes* is a book of divination whose basic text is attributed to very ancient times, possibly Early Chou or even earlier. It is based on the 64 hexagrams derived from the eight trigrams that are traditionally ascribed to the mythological Ruler Fu-hsi. (See Note 2 of this chapter.) Combining any two of the eight trigrams into diagrams of six lines each resulted in a total of 64 different combinations or hexagrams. Scholars differ on who formulated the hexagrams and who wrote the explanations to them. The identity of the author of the appendices that give further explanation of the hexagrams is also a matter of controversy. Most modern historians think the appendices could not be the work of Confucius or Confucius alone as is traditionally accepted. They probably were written by several persons who developed the basic ideas of the book by adding their own views.

During the Chou period, although the Shang methods of using bones of cattle or tortoise shells for divination were still in practice, a new method was devised. Stalks of milfoil were manipulated by the diviner in such a way as to produce a line-formation. Whichever of the 64 hexagrams of the *Book of Changes* it resembled most would probably have served as the basis of the interpretation.

The explanations of the hexagrams consist largely of words of wisdom or moral teaching. For that reason the *Book of Changes* was valued by the Chinese as an important source of instruction at ordinary times as well as in time of anxiety or .distress. For instance, the explanation of the Ch'ien Hexagram ☰ or the first of the hexagrams says,

> Use this time to further develop your inner strength. Refrain from taking direct action. Be observant. Think carefully. Ponder, contemplate. Consult with those wiser and more knowledgeable than yourself. Avoid extremes. Develop quiet confidence. It is a time for solitude and serenity, time to quietly cultivate and develop the four noble attitudes of firmness, strength, moderation, and justice.

See Frank J. MacHovec's translation of this explanation and the explanations of other hexagrams in *I Ching: The Book of Changes* (Mount Vernon, New York: Peter Pauper Press, 1971).

*The Book of History* is a collection of documents about government and institutions, including announcements, speeches, instructions, and reports said to have been made by the various rulers and their ministers from the time of the sage-kings of Yao, Shun, and Yü to that of Early Chou. It is said to have been edited by Confucius.

*The Book of Poetry* is a collection of 305 poems, mostly of the Early Chou period. Some of them are hymns used during ceremonies of sacrifice conducted by the kings or high ranking nobles. Others are songs to be sung at banquets or during meetings of the royalty or nobility. Still others are folk songs that include love songs and songs praising good government and satirizing, or complaining against, bad government officials. Confucius is supposed to have selected these poems from a larger number and edited them.

*The Ritual* is essentially a collection of texts on procedures and ceremonies of sacrificial and other public functions and rules of daily conduct, dating from Middle Chou down to Earlier Han (202 B.C.–A.D. 9). Its best-known section is the "Book of Rites." In this collection there is also an essay on music that is believed to be what is left of the lost *Book of Music*. Confucius is said to be the compiler and editor of parts of the collection.

*The Spring and Autumn Annals* is a history of the feudal state of Lu, the native state of Confucius. It also includes historical events that had taken place elsewhere but affected the state of Lu. This history, covering the period 772 to 481 B.C., is said to have been compiled by Confucius from various records in the archives of Lu. By the Earlier Han period, there were three commentaries—the *Tso-chuan*, the *Kung-yang*, and the *Ku-liang*—which are believed to be later additions, though the exact dates are controversial. The history of the state of Lu is both short and obscure. It is largely in the light of these commentaries that its history is interpreted.

8. There is no mention in any of the Five Classics of a creator of the universe. The impression is given that the universe was presumed to be there spontaneously.

9. H. G. Creel, *Chinese Thought from Confucius to Mao Tse-tung* (New York: New American Library, 1960), p. 23.

10. Two typical examples from the *Book of Poetry* as translated by James Legge in the *Chinese Classics*, vol. 4: *The Book of Poetry* (London: Oxford University Press, 1871), pp. 169-72, are as follows:

> K'an-k'an go his blows on the sandal trees,
> And he places what he hews on the river's bank,
> Whose waters flow clear and rippling.
> You sow not nor reap;—
> How do you get the produce of those three hundred farms?
> You do not follow the chase;—
> How do we see the badgers hanging up in your courtyards?
> O that superior man!
> He would not eat the bread of idleness!
>
> (First stanza of *Fah t'an*)

> Large rats! Large rats!
> Do not eat our millet,
> Three years have we had to do with you,
> And you have not been willing to show any regard for us.
> We will leave you,
> And go to that happy land.
> Happy land! Happy land!
> There shall we find our place.
>
> (First stanza of *Shih shoo*)

11. James Legge (trans.), *The Chinese Classics*, vol. 3: *The Book of Historical Documents* (London: Oxford University Press, 1865), pp. 392-93.

12. Wing-tsit Chan (trans. and comp.), *A Source Book in Chinese Philosophy* (Princeton, New Jersey: Princeton University Press, 1969), p. 13.

# 2

# Confucius

*T*he feudal period of Chou is known as the classical age of China, because almost all leading schools of Chinese thought arose during that period or to be more precise, during Middle Chou and Late Chou.[1] As mentioned previously, following Early Chou a few strong rulers of the feudal states gradually outpowered the king and fought among themselves for hegemony over the kingdom. It was a world of violence and disorder among the ruling class, as rulers were deposed or assassinated by their ministers and fathers were killed by their sons. The common people suffered, as they were burdened with heavy taxes and were frequently conscripted for war and hard labor. During these bad times, however, there was hardly any attempt at thought control and many schools of thought developed. Each school tried to win the favor of an individual feudal lord in order to change the Chinese world. The school of Confucius, though the least favored during his lifetime in Middle Chou, became the most influential during the Han period or about three centuries following his death. The life of Confucius, his education of students, his basic teachings, and his leading contributions to Chinese thought are discussed in the following sections.

## The Life of Confucius[2]

Confucius[2] (551-479 B.C.), the Latinized form of "K'ung Fu-tzu" or "Master K'ung,"[3] is celebrated in Chinese history as a great sage, a great teacher, and a great philosopher. He probably came from the family of a lesser noble of Lu,[4] a feudal state of the Chou Kingdom. His father, poor and insignificant, died when he was an infant, so Confucius had to make his own living and strive for his education at the same time. He was largely self-taught.

He probably had contact with the common people during his early youth, when he participated in manual labor. He witnessed their sufferings and had strong feelings for them. He believed the way to remove their misery and bring them happiness was to persuade the ruler to adopt a policy of serving their needs. Yet it has been said that his early positions in the government of his home state of Lu were too low for him to have had contact with the ruler. During his middle age he reached the position of Minister of Justice. In a few months' time he effected a wonderful renovation of the state. The duke of the feudal state of Ch'i began to fear that under the administration of Confucius, Lu would be so strong as to outpower Ch'i. So he sent the ruler of Lu a gift of beautiful women and fine horses. After accepting the gift, the ruler neglected the government and no longer listened to the advice of Confucius. As a result, Confucius resigned his position,[5] left Lu, and traveled from one feudal state to another for almost 13 years looking for a ruler who would accept his advice. He failed to find one.

He was disappointed but not bitter. He spent the last years of his life teaching in Lu, as he believed it was the will of Heaven for him to educate his students so that in the future they would succeed in the same pursuit. It was said that he taught altogether some 3000 students among whom 72 were known for their superior character and behavior. A few among the 72 did succeed in persuading various feudal lords to change or modify their government policies for the well-being of the people.

## Education of Students

Confucius was probably the first to establish teaching as a profession in China.[6] He broke the tradition of his time that education was the special privilege of the ruling class or men of noble birth known as "chun-tzu." He taught men of all stations in life, so long as they had the desire and ability to learn.[7] As a result, he introduced a new definition of "chun-tzu," which literally means "the son of a ruler," and which was used to imply something like the English "gentleman." "Chun-tzu," sometimes translated as "superior man," was theoretically expected to be a man superior by birth and also superior in character and behavior. It was Confucius who waived the requisite of birth. He redefined chun-tzu as any man of superior character and behavior. Although he did not give a clear-cut answer to the question of whether human nature was good or evil, he believed that men were by nature nearly alike[8] and, with few exceptions,[9] could be educated along the path of chun-tzu. His ultimate goal in education was therefore to produce chun-tzu and so to change society and government for the well-being of the people who were largely uneducated during his time.

It is evident that he took morality as the center of education. His curriculum and method of teaching were directed toward the cultivation of his students' character and behavior according to his code of ethics. The exact curriculum that he adopted for his students is not known, but the Six Disciplines[10]—the *Book of Changes,* the *Book of History,* the *Book of Poetry,* the *Book of Rites,* the *Book of Music,* and the *Spring and Autumn Annals*—seem to have taken an important place. These classics, formerly taught only to princes and the sons of nobles, were now introduced to his students with his new interpretations. In studying the *Book of Changes,* he emphasized the underlying moral instruction rather than divination. In teaching the *Book of History* and the *Book of Poetry,* he stressed their ethical significance. In discussing the *Book of Rites,* he paid special attention to the spirit of respect rather than the form of the ceremony. In talking about the *Book of Music,* he presented the ethical concept behind the melody. Likewise, in commenting on the *Spring and Autumn Annals* (which is essentially a history of Lu), he pointed out the moral lessons to be learned from it.

His method of teaching seems to have been entirely informal. There is no mention in the Lun Yü or *Analects of Confucius* or in any other reliable record of his holding classes, or giving specific assignments or examinations. Probably his students were expected to study certain classics themselves and then discuss key passages or difficult passages with him. They were not expected to sit rigidly and give their full attention to him when he talked or raised questions.[11] He preferred to create an easy atmosphere for the discussion of serious matters. He was respectful of the young as well as the older students, encouraging them to think for themselves. Instead of telling them what he thought was absolute truth and forcing them to follow it, he used his own opinions to illustrate the way toward truth, along which they should seek the truth themselves.[12] To impart knowledge was therefore a small part of his function as a teacher. His larger motive was to promote the growth of the mind, the development of character, and the improvement of the behavior of his students according to their individual differences in intelligence and capacity. He observed each student carefully and was able to evaluate the achievement of each.[13]

He gave answers to all questions of his students except those concerning physical exploits, weird things, disorders of nature, and spirits.[14] He did not explain exactly why he refused to go into these. Probably he wanted his students to concentrate on what was morally constructive and not pay attention to what could be achieved by mere physical strength or what was related to the many superstitions of his time. He himself participated in sacrifices to pay respect to the spirits as if they were present.[15] On the other hand, he told his students that other than on occasions of sacrifice they should, as a matter of wisdom, keep their distance from the spirits. It was more important to devote themselves to the duties they owed to the people.[16] Since ancestors should be remembered, it was correct to pay them respect as if they were alive; but sacrifice to them and other spirits was the expression of respect only.

He participated in the sacrifice to Heaven for the sake of reverence, but he also believed in Heaven as the guiding Providence. "Heaven" to him expressed the Western concept of "God"—the Almighty. He thought one's fulfillment as a man came from acting in accordance with the will of Heaven. It was Heaven who had created the moral order and guided men to follow. When a man followed the moral order, he followed the will of Heaven. He believed that Heaven instructed him to cure the ills of the Chinese world and he tried in every possible way to fulfill that mission.[17] Although he never actively discussed Heaven or spirits with his students, he taught them to follow the will of Heaven. His life coincided with the Western saying, "Do your best and leave the rest to God."

We may conclude from studying the *Analects of Confucius* that his success as a teacher and an educator came from the good example he set for his students. He first practiced what he intended to teach and then taught what he had already practiced.[18] His manner was gentle yet firm, dignified but not harsh, polite but easy.[19] He was always anxious to learn and patient in teaching others. It was therefore not surprising for his students to think of him as a sage or a man of perfect virtue and wisdom as well as a good teacher. Being modest, he denied that he was a sage.[20]

## Basic Teachings

Since he aimed at making chun-tzu or superior men out of his students, he talked often about the elements that constituted a chun-tzu. Once he said a chun-tzu must possess "jen,"[21] wisdom, and courage.[22] He had many discussions with his students as to what "jen" was. Sometimes it was defined as the virtue of love or loving others.[23] More often it was defined as virtue in its entirety. For instance, Confucius once answered a student by saying that jen was the denial of self and response to the right and proper.[24] Another time he said a man of jen must possess kindness, breadth (generosity of soul or forgiveness), good faith, diligence, and courtesy.[25] In fact, when we analyze the many discussions on jen, we find that the term also covers loyalty, filial piety, brotherliness, respectfulness, justice, sincerity, and all kinds of different individual virtues required of a person in his relations with his family, society, and government. Jen, the center of Confucius' philosophy, therefore means complete human virtue.[26]

The practice of jen meant deep concern for others. Confucius said a man must help others in order to get established as he would like himself to get established, and one must help others to succeed as he would desire himself to succeed.[27] He also said one must not do to others what he would not like others to do to him.[28]

Confucius regarded the practice of jen as so important that the man of jen should not seek to live at the expense of injuring his jen. He would even sacrifice his life to preserve his jen.[29] A chun-tzu would preserve his jen rather than his life, when it became a matter of choice.[30]

Outwardly a chun-tzu must act according to "li," which literally means rites or ceremonial acts. It underlies the idea of what is proper, or the fitness of things, and what reason calls for in the performance of duties toward superior beings, and be- tween man and man. It covers all rules of propriety, not only those in connection with formal ceremonies but also those regarding good manners and daily conduct. The rules of propri- ety must be practiced with a natural ease.[31] They must be in keeping with circumstances. That is to say, they are not to be followed purely as a matter of conforming to tradition. Reason and good taste must dictate their change or modification accord- ing to circumstances. Above all, there must be a true spirit of respect behind the acts of ceremony and good manners. Without such a spirit, the acts would become only the pretense of li.

Music, which was traditionally used to accompany various rites, was also regarded by Confucius as important. When it was performed, it was supposed to reflect the virtue and sentiment of its composer and to inspire its listeners accordingly. For exam- ple, Confucius admired the music made by the Sage-King Shun as perfectly beautiful and perfectly good. He thought the music of King Wu of the Chou was also perfectly beautiful in melody, but because of its martial character he would not call it perfectly good.[32] He was so carried away by the excellent music of Shun that, after listening to it, he lost the taste for meat or good food for a period of three months.[33]

The playing of and listening to good music also constituted a part of personal cultivation. When one revealed his feeling of happiness or sorrow through music, he achieved a kind of emotional balance or harmony within himself. Confucius used to play the lute and sing. It has been recorded in the *Analects* that when he cried at a funeral, he did not sing the rest of the day.[34]

In terms of personal conduct, all in all, Confucius stood for the Mean[35]—comparable to the Greek Golden Mean, never to go to extremes.

Confucius also laid down some basic principles in government for his students. He believed in government by moral persuasion rather than the severity of law.[36] His ideal ruler was the "sage-king"—the man of both virtue and wisdom who would not only do good for the people but also inspire and lead them to be good. Since ideal rulers were rare under the traditional practice of hereditary succession, he, following his own political failure, tried to educate his students to become virtuous and capable ministerial candidates. He expected them or some of them to influence the policy of some of the rulers and to be selected for the administrative functions of a good government.

As to what was meant by a "good" government, Confucius believed it must be a government which made the people who were close to it happy and which attracted those who lived far off.[37] In government, the people, not the ruler or the state, should come first. Prosperity and education constituted the happiness of the people.[38] The ruler and his officials must have love and concern for the people. In conducting the government, they must adopt a policy of economy in expenditure. In dealing with the people, they must be generous, honest, sincere, and just. Dignified but not fierce, they themselves mut be diligent and serious in their work at all times.[39]

## Leading Contributions to Chinese Thought

Confucius thought of himself as a transmitter of ancient Chinese teachings rather than as a creator of Chinese thought. In fact, he was much more than a transmitter. He was a creator through being a transmitter.[40] His interpretation of the Six Disciplines, as discussed previously, proves that he was not one who simply imparted knowledge of the ancient classics. He integrated the underlying concepts and principles from these classics and established a system of thought that embodied many of his own ideas.

Confucius' idea that in education there were no class distinctions[41] was unheard of during the feudal period. His respect for individuals, young as well as old; his encouragement of his students to conduct themselves according to the ethical code of the chun-tzu; his insistence that they think for themselves and be their own masters; all these are in keeping with modern concepts of education. Furthermore, he made serving the needs of the people the responsibility of the better-educated. The promotion of individual initiative and development was not for personal fulfillment alone; it was also for the collective good. Such was his lofty goal in education.

If we presume that Confucius compiled a code of ethics from scattered ancient Chinese teachings, we should also notice that he modified and developed certain aspects of such teachings as he did so. On the one hand he stood by the old teaching of loyalty to the ruler and filial piety to the father or parents; on the other, he believed the ruler must act like a good ruler and the father, a good father, if loyalty from the subject and filial piety from the son were to be expected in return.[42] The head of the government and that of the household must bear alike the major burdens of moral responsibility and must serve as good examples. Furthermore, he taught that loyalty should ultimately be given to moral principles rather than to any person. His teaching that one should be willing to sacrifice his life for the preservation of his moral principles was comparable to the Christian teaching that one's life could and should be sacrificed in defense of one's faith.

While the ancient Chinese classics taught men to imitate the good in history and to avoid the evil, Confucius went further. He thought lessons could also be learned from one's own circle. "Even when walking in a party of no more than three," he said, "I can always be certain of learning from those I am with. There will be good qualities that I can select for imitation and bad ones that will teach me what requires correction in myself."[43]

Although Confucius did not actively denounce feudalism as an institution, many of his political ideas were in fact antifeudal. His ideas that in government the people should come first and that the use of moral persuasion rather than severe punishment should be the government policy were both contrary to the feudal practice of his time. His emphasis on moral persuasion seems to have influenced the Chinese in their development of a tradition of preferring moral persuasion through arbitration rather than recourse to legal process in the settlement of non-criminal disputes.

Confucius' belief that sacrifice was an expression of respect, rather than a kind of barter transaction with Heaven, or with any other spiritual being in order to obtain blessings or avoid calamities, influenced his students and followers in later periods. He turned the attention of his students from superstition to the active building of a "paradise on earth." He emphasized the here-and-now and refused to speculate about what was beyond. Yet this ideal here-and-now could not come about without following the will of Heaven, and the will of Heaven was to follow the moral order. In this way, he imparted a religious connotation to morality or his code of ethics, although he never established a religion of his own.[44]

As a philosopher, Confucius lived up to the best of his teachings. His philosophy was at once his way of life. The Chinese belief in the inseparability of philosophy and life probably started from him.

Confucius and his teachings were little respected by the men of his time. For centuries the school of Confucius remained one among many rival schools of philosophy. Not until the Han period (202 B.C.–A.D. 220) did Confucianism become the predominant philosophy of the nation. What was known as Confucianism at this time was, however, not quite the same as the teachings of Confucius. They had been modified, perverted, and even distorted, as will be discussed later.

### Notes

1. See ch. 1 for the division of this period into Early Chou, Middle Chou, and Late Chou.

2. There was no complete record of the life of Confucius during or shortly after his lifetime. Later records vary and their authenticity is in great part doubtful. The brief traditional account of his life here presented in part comes from the Lun Yü or *Analects of Confucius,* a record of his conversations and activities probably compiled by students of his students. It is regarded by many scholars as the most reliable source available.

3. His given name was Ch'iu. Because of the Chinese traditional respect for him, the title used in referring to him in Chinese is K'ung Fu-tzu or K'ung-

tzu. Both *Fu-tzu* and *Tzu* mean Master. The Chinese tradition is for the family name to come first.

4. Lu is in the modern province of Shantung.

5. The Lun Yü or *Analects*, 18:4 (to stand for Book 18: ch. 4). Later references will be indicated in the same way.

There are several English translations of the *Analects*. Two that are frequently used are the translation by James Legge (entitled the *Confucian Analects*) published in different editions, and that by Arthur Waley (entitled the *Analects of Confucius*) published in London and New York. Since each scholar-translator had his own insights, it would be helpful to read both translations.

6. Yu-lan Fung, *A History of Chinese Philosophy*, vol. 1 (Derke Bodde trans.) (Princeton, New Jersey: Princeton University Press, 1952), pp. 52-53.

7. *The Analects*, 7:8.

8. Ibid., 17:2.

9. These exceptions were the extremely good and wise and the extremely bad and stupid. See ibid., 17:3.

10. At the time of Confucius there was probably a *Book of Music*, which together with the other Five Classics, comprised the Six Disciplines. It is not known when and how a good portion of the *Book of Music* got lost. What was left of it was only an essay on music collected under the *Ritual*. So what is known as the Five Classics is essentially the leftover of the Six Disciplines. See Note 7 of ch.1 for further details.

11. For example, when Confucius asked what were the individual wishes of his students, his student Tien, playing on the lute, did not stop playing until it was his turn to answer the question. See the *Analects*, 11:25.

12. See ibid., 9:22, 2:15, and 15:15. See also the comment on it as "intellectual democracy" in H. G. Creel, *Chinese Thought from Confucius to Mao Tse-tung* (New York: New American Library of World Literature, 1960), p. 44. Professor Creel is probably the best American interpreter of Confucius and Confucius' teachings.

13. See the *Analects*, 5:7 and 6:6 for Confucius' evaluation of several of his students with respect to their capacities and specific abilities to serve the government.

14. Ibid., 7:20.

15. Ibid., 3:12.

16. Ibid., 6:20.

17. Ibid., 9:5 and 2:4.

18. Ibid., 2:13.

19. Ibid., 7:37.

20. Ibid., 7:33.

21. The conventional way of writing the Chinese character for jen is 仁. It is composed of two parts. The left part 亻 means man and the right part 二 means two. It did not have any convincing interpretation until Professor Chaoying Fang argued from the Korean source that the right part of jen was probably a mistake for 上 which means top or above. The character

for jen therefore implies what is achieved by the man above or the superior man—the chun-tzu. See Chaoying Fang, *The Asami Library: A Descriptive Catalogue* (Berkeley, California: University of California Press, 1969), p. viii.

22. *The Analects,* 14:30.

23. Ibid., 12:22.

24. Ibid., 12:1. The translation here is taken from Yu-lan Fung, *A History of Chinese Philosophy,* p. 70.

25. *The Analects,* 17:6.

26. Yu-lan Fung, *A History of Chinese Philosophy,* p. 72.

27. *The Analects,* 6:28.

28. Ibid., 15:23.

29. Ibid., 15:8.

30. It was said that when the First Emperor of Ch'in of the third century B.C. gave an order to burn books of all schools of thought other than those of the Legalists (which he favored), a number of followers of Confucius criticized the order as wrong and pleaded with the Emperor to change his mind. Instead, the Emperor threatened to bury them alive should they refuse to retract their criticism. They refused. So they were buried alive.

31. *The Analects,* 1:12.

32. Ibid., 3:25.

33. Ibid., 7:13.

34. Ibid., 7:9.

35. Ibid., 6:27 and 11:15.

36. Ibid., 2:3 and 12:19.

37. Ibid., 13:16.

38. Ibid., 13:9.

39. Ibid., 1:5 and 20:1 and 2.

40. Yu-lan Fung, *A History of Chinese Philosophy,* p. 65.

41. *The Analects,* 15:38.

42. Ibid., 12:11.

43. Ibid., 7:21 as translated by Arthur Waley in his *The Analects of Confucius,* p. 127. The Waley translation of this passage is the most vivid.

44. Although in A.D. 59 Emperor Ming of the Later Han dynasty (25-220 A.D.) started the Confucian cult by ordering sacrificial offerings to be made to the sage in the government schools, such offerings did not make Confucius a god or his teachings a popular faith in the eyes of the Chinese people. As pointed out by Professor Liu, "The salient fact remains that Master K'ung (Confucius) did not make any claim to godship, nor did he teach a faith that was supernatural and sanctimonious. This clearly indicates that Master K'ung originally had nothing to do with religion. Moreover, despite the later acts of homage heaped on him, there has never been evolved a K'ung (Confucian) priesthood with all its paraphernalia." See Liu Wu-chi, *A Short History of Confucian Philosophy* (New York: Dell, 1955), pp. 183–84.

# 3

# Mo Tzu

*A*mong the many schools of thought developed during the period of Chou, Moism was the next most important school after Confucianism. From the fifth to the third century B.C., Confucianism and Moism dominated the intellectual scene, competing for influence and attacking each other virgorously.[1]

## The Life of Mo Tzu

A few years after the death of Confucius, Mo Ti, known as "Mo Tzu" or "Master Mo" (ca. 470-391 B.C.) was born in the feudal state of Sung or Lu, Confucius' native state.[2] Very little is known about his life. The ancient classics provided his education. Probably he studied at first with some scholars of the Confucian school. Later he came to believe that Confucianism was not the way to eliminate the social ills of his day, so he established his own school and became the leading opponent of the Confucianists.

He probably served for a while as a high minister of the feudal state of Sung. Then he traveled through many other feudal states, trying to make their rulers accept his doctrine of "universal love,"[3] and urging them to stop waging wars. He had little success in either aim. Whenever he failed to prevent a ruler from attacking the state of another ruler, he would bring his followers to help defend the state under attack. In time he and his followers became experts in the techniques of defensive warfare. He had about 300 followers who formed a close-knit and well-disciplined group under his direction. He led a life of self-sacrifice in the service of others, true to his belief in "universal love."

## Basic Teachings

The pattern of thought and the standard of action of Mo Tzu were completely utilitarian. To him the value of anything or any doctrine depended on the benefit it could bring to the people and state. The greatest of all benefits were wealth and populousness. Everything that could further such growth was to be encouraged; anything that tended to injure or retard such growth had to be removed. He believed that all decorative elements in clothing, houses, and other objects of utility should be avoided in order to eliminate needless expenditure.[4] He condemned elaborate funerals as burying wealth in the ground, and decried long periods of mourning for the dead as time wasted that could have been used for the increase of wealth and population. The state was impoverished thereby.[5] He was against music, because it brought no immediate material benefit to the people. Furthermore, he believed that the musical entertainments of the aristocracy wasted wealth that came from taxation of the common people.[6] He regarded early marriage as a good way of increasing population and condemned warfare for its opposite effect.[7]

He especially condemned warfare of aggression, asserting that it was unprofitable and destructive. In preparing for a campaign, the aggressor state would spend a great deal of time and money. Its officials, high and low, would necessarily ignore the ordinary affairs of government. Its people, largely farmers, would have no time to reap or sow. When the war broke out, the aggressor state, like the state being attacked, would lose trained fighting men. The common people of both sides would be forced to abandon their occupations. States at his time, he argued, were in need of more people, not more land. To go to war with each other over land and to succeed only in doing injury to each other's people meant to destroy what the states did not have enough of for the sake of what they had in excess.[8]

It would be much more profitable to substitute good government for aggressive warfare.[9]

A good government was a government headed by an enlightened ruler who would practice universal love. He would think of his people first and of himself last. He would bring them all kinds of material benefits. He would feed them when they were hungry, clothe them when they were cold, nourish them when they were sick, and bury them when they died.[10] He would love all the people in the same way and to the same degree that he loved himself. Mo Tzu condemned the Confucian idea that love for all should start from the family and that in the family the parents should come first. He believed that one should love other men's parents as if they were one's own. Only when a man did this would other men, in return, love his parents like their own. One who loved and helped others would be loved and helped by others.[11] "If everyone in the world would practice universal love . . . then the whole world would enjoy peace and good order."[12] Mo Tzu favored the suppression of all emotions, including the romantic concept of love. Universal love in his definition was a function of the mind rather than the heart. It demanded an exchange of love for love and benefit for benefit. It was a doctrine of "enlightened self-interest."[13]

Mo Tzu knew that he could not expect all the people to practice universal love voluntarily, for he believed human nature to be like pure silk and its goodness or evil dependent entirely upon what it was dyed with. Just to "dye" the people with the doctrine of universal love would not be enough. Because of their short-sightedness, it was very difficult to make them see the benefits of his doctrine and substitute it for what was harmful. So he stressed the need for a variety of sanctions that would induce men to love one another.[14]

The most important sanctions were religious and political. He held that Heaven, the Supreme Being, rewarded people who practiced universal love and punished the perverse. It was the will of Heaven for the ruler and his subject to love universally. He claimed that the ancient sage-kings Yü, T'ang, Wen, and Wu were honored by Heaven with the throne and the possession of the world because they obeyed the will of Heaven and practiced universal love. On the other hand, evil kings of olden times, like

Chieh, Chou, Yu, and Li who opposed the will of Heaven were punished by Heaven with dethronement and death before their time.[15] Reward or punishment cannot be avoided by anybody.

Political sanction was to come from the ruler or his government. In the far-off beginning of human life, Mo Tzu said, there was neither law nor government. Everyone decided matters according to his own standard of right and wrong. As a result, there were disorder and wars. Then the most qualified man in the land was chosen by Heaven to be the ruler known as the Son of Heaven. The Son of Heaven selected qualified men to be his leading ministers; these leading ministers in turn selected qualified men to be their subordinates; and so on, down to the lowest ranking officials of the various localities. The Son of Heaven (following the will of Heaven) set a unified standard of right and wrong and enforced it among the people through his government officials of all echelons. Rewards and punishments were used to force compliance. Peace and order were thereby effected in the ruler's domain.[16] Universal love, which represented the highest standard of right, therefore would be enforced by the government whose authority is justified because it came from Heaven.

## Basic Differences in the Teachings of Confucius and Mo Tzu

Both Confucius and Mo Tzu were deeply concerned over the suffering of the people in the grip of war, disorder, and poverty, but their ideas and methods for eliminating suffering and serving the people's needs were quite different. Confucius believed that the ruler, for love of the people, should first of all bring them prosperity. This was comparable to Mo Tzu's idea that material benefits were to be provided by the ruler through the practice of universal love. Confucius, however, believed that the ruler must provide the people with education, something Mo Tzu did not mention.

Confucius believed that the ruler should use predominantly moral persuasion to lead men to be good. He prescribed no system of government. He trusted that the ruler would employ virtuous and wise ministers whose administration would work for the well-being of the people. Mo Tzu held that the ruler must set a unified standard of right and wrong and enforce it among the people through an authoritarian government and the lure of reward and the threat of punishment.

As far as love for all was concerned, Confucius seems to have believed it more reasonable to expect men to start from love for their parents and other members of their families, thereafter progressing to love for others in society, in the state, and in the world. Thus would be realized his ultimate goal of world brotherhood. Mo Tzu was for loving others as one loved oneself. Since he did not believe it was the nature of men to do so, he emphasized both religious and political sanctions to compel the people to practice it. Because he favored the suppression of all emotions, his universal love had to come from the mind. The love of Confucius' way of thought proceeded from the heart. Universal love was to exchange love for love and benefit for benefit. Confucius' idea of love was that it was practiced for its own sake and therefore expected nothing in return.

Confucius stood for the Mean. He believed in frugality or moderation in expenditure, but not to the extreme of Mo Tzu. Nor was Confucius purely utilitarian. He was well aware of the people's material need for food, clothing, and shelter, but also appreciated the immaterial values in music and rites and various forms of art. Mo Tzu took these to be merely causes for waste of wealth.

Confucius favored flexibility. Once he established a basic code of ethics, he expected the details to be worked out according to one's reason, good taste, and the given circumstances. He encouraged independent thinking and development of individual initiative. Mo Tzu stood for complete uniformity. As Hsün Tzu, a leading follower of Confucius, put it, Mo Tzu had no vision regarding individuality.[17]

Moism or the teachings of Mo Tzu was no longer a leading school of thought during the Han period (202 B.C.-A.D. 220) at the time when Confucianism became prominent.

**Notes**

1. Wing-tsit Chan (trans. and comp.), *A Source Book in Chinese Philosophy* (Princeton, New Jersey: Princeton University Press, 1963), p. 211.

2. Ibid., p. 212.

3. See p. 31 on the explanation of universal love.

4. *Mo Tzu: Basic Writings* (Burton Watson, trans.) (New York: Columbia University Press, 1963), pp. 62-63.

5. Ibid., pp. 67-70. Mo Tzu exaggerated to some extent as is indicated by Note 1 of ibid., p. 68.

6. Ibid., pp. 110-11.

7. Ibid., pp. 63-64.

8. Ibid., pp. 54-55.

9. Ibid., p. 60.

10. Ibid., p. 43.

11. Ibid., pp. 46-47.

12. *The Ethical and Political Works of Motse* (Y. P. Mei, trans.) (London: Probsthain, 1929), p. 80.

13. H. G. Creel, *Chinese Thought from Confucius to Mao Tse-tung* (New York: New American Library, 1960), p. 54.

14. Yu-lan Fung, *A History of Chinese Philosophy,* vol. I (Derk Bodde, trans.) (Princeton, New Jersey: Princeton University Press, 1952), p. 96.

15. *Mo Tzu: Basic Writings,* pp. 80-81.

16. Ibid., pp. 34-38.

17. Yu-lan Fung, *A History of Chinese Philosophy,* p. 102.

# 4

# The Taoists: Lao Tzu
# And Chuang Tzu

*T*aoism, the philosophy of the Taoist school, is a mystical philosophy of the Chinese. Its influence on the Chinese mind is only second to that of Confucianism or the philosophy of the Confucian school. Lao Tzu and Chuang Tzu are known as the founders of the Taoist school. *The Lao Tzu* and *The Chuang Tzu,* books that bear their names, are supposed to have been written by them respectively. Modern scholars, however, believe that both books are collections of Taoist writings and sayings, each made by different persons at different times, rather than the single work of any one person.[1] *The Lao Tzu,* also known as *Tao-te Ching,* is concise, cryptic, and paradoxical. It consists of poetical passages and prose interpretations and commentaries. *The Chuang Tzu,* more skeptical and mystical, is written in prose.

### The Lives of Lao Tzu and Chuang Tzu

Little is known about either Lao Tzu or Chuang Tzu. According to the Chinese traditional accounts, Lao Tzu lived during the time of Confucius (551-479 B.C.) and Chuang Tzu, during the time of Mencius (372-289 B.C.). Modern scholars believe that both masters lived after Confucius. The dates and details of the life of Lao Tzu are uncertain. Chuang Tzu, whose given name was Chou, probably lived during the latter half of the fourth century, B.C.[2] He probably was a native of the feudal state of Sung and served as an official of unknown rank or capacity.[3]

## The Basic Teachings of Lao Tzu and Chuang Tzu

The teachings of Lao Tzu are based on a great, underlying principle called the Tao, from which the name of his school originates. The Chinese character "tao" literally means a road, or path, or way. Confucius used it to denote the right way of action in human affairs. Lao Tzu, the first man who gave it its metaphysical concept, used it to denote the Way of ultimate Reality. It signifies the original undifferentiated Reality from which the universe evolved, and it also refers to the way the whole world of nature operates.[4] In other words, Tao is "the source of creation"[5] or the source of all beings. It existed before the universe and gave birth to all things that constitute the universe. It represents and regulates all things in the universe. Since it stands for the totality of all things, it is equivalent to what some Western philosophers have called "the absolute."[6]

The goal of the Taoist is "to be one with the Tao,"[7] to be in harmony with the order of nature. Nature (or the way nature operates) is described as simple, spontaneous, tranquil, content, and nonstriving.[8] It produces without the desire for ownership. It bestows without the intention for reward. It rules without the claim for lordship. The Taoist, in his pursuit of unity with the Tao, must possess the qualities of nature and get along as nature does. He must live a life of simplicity. That is, he must preserve his natural and primitive qualities of plainness, honesty, and sincerity and put away the artificial manners of civilization. He must practice "wu-wei,"[9] which literally means nonaction but actually refers to taking no action that is not natural or spontaneous. He must also practice the precept of tranquility or silence, talking as little as possible. He achieves, but does not claim any achievement for himself. He gives without the wish for return. He does things without the desire for his own gain. He has a good understanding of what is and is not feasible or suitable for himself. He knows how far he can go and does not strain after what is beyond his own capacity to reach. He knows when to stop after he begins and he is contented with what he has achieved. He believes it is not how far one has gone or how much one has achieved but how contented one is with his own achievement that determines his peace of mind and therefore happiness.

In government, the ideal ruler described in *The Lao Tzu* is one who leads the people back to the state of primitive simplicity. He himself must possess the virtues of mercy or compassion, frugality, and humility.[10] He must not overtax the people or oppress them in any way. He must not make them fight his wars of political or territorial expansion. He must not live in luxury. On the one hand, he must keep the people well-fed. On the other, he must lead them to be humble, to cherish honesty, to abandon selfish desires, and to shun deceit, cunning, and artifice. When the people preserve their genuine goodness, there is no need for the teaching of "love and righteousness";[11] and so such teaching should be discarded.

*The Chuang Tzu* shares with *The Lao Tzu* the metaphysical concept of the Tao and the goal of the Taoist as mentioned previously. *The Chuang Tzu,* however, advocates a different way of dealing with the world. While *The Lao Tzu* makes proposals to reform the individual and the society, and eventually to free the world from its ills, *The Chuang Tzu* teaches how to free oneself spiritually from the world. In a world dominated by chaos, suffering, and absurdity, man must discard the conventional values in order to set his mind free and therefore free himself from the world. Things are what they are called. Right and wrong are just words that man may apply to the same thing. Ills are ills, because man recognized them as such. Man's worry over and fear of ills comes from the web of values created by himself. Once he discards his web of values, he will cease to label things as good or bad, desirable or undesirable. Man-made ills such as war, poverty, and injustice will disappear. Natural ills such as disease and death[12] will not hurt or bother his mind. They will be accepted quietly as inevitable parts of the course of nature. When man achieves freedom of his mind, he sets himself free from the world.[13]

While *The Lao Tzu* believes that the ideal ruler leads the people back to the state of primitive simplicity, *The Chuang Tzu* advocates government of the people through "nongovernment," or letting the people alone. The natures of different men or things are not the same, and each individual has his own special likings. Men and things can reach the state of harmony with nature and therefore happiness through following their own natures. There is neither necessity nor reason to establish political and social institutions for the enforcement of a uniform standard of conduct, as is favored by the Confucian sage. In so doing, it would be like the story of the Marquis of Lu who, for the love of a seabird, fed it and treated it in the same way as he did himself, and found the bird dead three days later (ch. 18 of *The Chuang Tzu*). To constrain different men to a forced uniformity will, therefore, result in harming them. When they are let alone, good order and peace, which they generally desire, will result spontaneously.[14]

*The Chuang Tzu* stresses that Tao is the basic undivided unity in which all the contradictions and distinctions of existence are ultimately resolved, and that Tao has infinite possibilities that are beyond man's knowledge to understand. Man, therefore, should follow the natural course and leave to Tao to bring all things into unity and to be the equalizer. He who comprehends and dwells in the underlying unity of Tao finds "enjoyment in the realm of the infinite."[15] Chuang Tzu's sage (or man of virtue and wisdom) is, therefore, one who withdraws into the life of a hermit and contemplates the universe; he is not a man of social and political achievements.

Evidently, the philosophy of Lao Tzu, rather than that of Chuang Tzu, is closer to Confucianism. Despite their difference in methods of reform, both Lao Tzu and Confucius aimed at reforming this world here and now, whereas Chuang Tzu sought to rise above the world and become transcendental.

The philosophy of *The Lao Tzu* plays a more important role in Chinese thought than that of *The Chuang Tzu*. Since the fifth century, the teachings of *The Chuang Tzu* have never been propagated by any outstanding scholar. On the other hand, the impact of *The Chuang Tzu* on the religion of Buddhism has been great, especially in the development of the Ch'an (Zen) school. *The Chuang Tzu* has also been a main source of inspiration in Chinese landscape painting and poetry. Furthermore, it helped develop the school known as Neo-Confucianism during the eleventh and twelfth centuries.[16]

## Notes

1. Yu-lan Fung, *A Short History of Chinese Philosophy* (Derk Bodde, ed.) (New York, 1948), p. 65.

2. Herrlee G. Creel, *What Is Taoism? And Other Studies in Chinese Cultural History* (Chicago: University of Chicago Press, 1970), p. 12.

3. Chuang Tzu, *Chuang Tzu: Basic Writings* (Burton Watson, trans.) (New York: Columbia University Press, 1964), p. 1.

4. Lao Tzu, *Tao Te Ching (The Way of Life: Lao Tzu)* (Raymond B. Blakney, trans.) (New York: The New American Library, 1955), p. 37.

5. Ibid., line 3 of the poetical passage of ch. 1, p. 53.

6. See H. G. Creel, *Chinese Thought from Confucius to Mao Tse-tung* (New York: New American Library, 1964), p. 87. Also see Max Kaltenmark, *Lao Tzu and Taoism* (Roger Greaves, trans.) (Stanford, Calif.: Stanford University Press, 1969), p. 35 and Arthur Waley, *The Way and Its Power: A Study of The Tao-te Ching and Its Place in Chinese Thought* (New York: Grove, 1958), p. 163.

7. See the third line from the bottom of the poetical passage of ch. 16 of *Tao-te Ching* as translated in Wm. Theodore de Bary, Wing-tsit Chan, and Burton Watson (comps.), *Sources of Chinese Tradition,* vol. I (New York: Columbia University Press, 1964), p. 55.

8. See translations of poetical passages of ch. 28, 51, 61, 33, and 8 of *Tao-te Ching* in Wing-tsit Chan (trans. and comp.), *A Source Book in Chinese Philosophy* (Princeton, N.J.: Princeton University Press, 1969), pp. 154, 163, 168, 156, and 143 respectively. The translation of the poetical passage of ch. 8, "Water benefits all things generously and is without strife" in de Bary, Chan, and Watson, *Sources of Chinese Tradition,* p. 53, seems to be more expressive than Chan's "Water is good; it benefits all things and does not compete with them."

9. For the interpretation of "wu-wei," see translations of poetical passages of ch. 37, 43, and 48 of *Tao-te Ching* in Chan, *A Source Book in Chinese Philosophy,* pp. 158, 161, and 162 respectively.

10. See poetical passage in ch. 67 of *Tao-te Ching* as translated in de Bary, Chan, and Watson, *Sources of Chinese Tradition,* pp. 60-61.

11. See translations of poetical passages of ch. 18 and 19 of *Tao-te Ching* in ibid., p. 55. "Love (or humanity) and righteousness" was supposed to be the best teaching of the then-Confucianists.

12. See the story of Chuang Tzu—how upon the death of his wife he, instead of mourning, drummed upon an inverted bowl and sang—in Arthur Waley, *Three Ways of Thought in Ancient China* (New York: Doubleday), pp. 6-7. Reprint of the 1939 Allen & Unwin edition (London).

13. Chuang Tzu, *Chuang Tzu: Basic Writings,* pp. 3-4.

14. See Yu-lan Fung, *A History of Chinese Philosophy,* vol. 1 (Derk

Bodde, trans.) (Princeton, N.J.: Princeton University Press, 1952), pp. 226-30.

15. See ibid., p. 231; see also de Bary, Chan, and Watson, *Sources of Chinese Tradition,* p. 73.

16. Wing-tsit Chan, *A Source Book in Chinese Philosophy,* pp. 178-79.

# 5

# Prominent Followers of Confucius: Mencius and Hsün Tzu

*T*here were many prominent followers of Confucius during and after his lifetime and several well-known works are attributed to them.[1] Here only Mencius and Hsün Tzu will be discussed, because these two masters developed the thought of Confucius along quite different lines. As a result, two main branches of Confucianism emerged.

*The Mencius* and *The Hsün Tzu,* works that bear the author's names, are our major sources of knowledge about their lives and teachings. *The Mencius,* probably put together by his students, includes the sayings and conversations of Mencius with his students and feudal lords, and his refutation of doctrines of other schools of philosophy prevalent at his time. *The Hsün Tzu* is a collection of writings by Hsün Tzu himself.

## The Life of Mencius (ca. 372-289 B.C.)

Mencius is the Latinized form of "Meng Tzu" or "Master Meng," who was the best-known among all followers of Confucius. He figures in Chinese history as the "Second Sage" or the "Man of Virtue and Wisdom." He was born in the feudal state of Ch'i, adjacent to Confucius' home state of Lu, at a time when the six or seven larger feudal states of the Chou kingdom, after swallowing up the smaller states, were fighting among themselves for supremacy. He learned the teachings of Confucius from the students of that master's grandson, Tzu Ssu. Like Confucius, Mencius spent most of his life in search of a ruler who would take his advice that government must be for the greater good of the people. Unable to find such a ruler, he spent the last years of his life as a devoted teacher.

## Basic Teachings of Mencius

The basic moral teachings of Mencius are little different from those of Confucius. However, in the course of trying to interpret the teachings of Confucius, especially the virtues which were not clearly defined by the latter, he injected some of his own ideas.

Like Confucius, he believed jen should be the leading virtue of a chun-tzu or superior man. In addition, he laid stress on "i," which he interpreted as righteousness or moral duty or responsibility. "'Jen' (the 'jen' of Confucius which includes all moral qualities of humanity)," he said, "is man's heart and 'i' is man's path."[2] A man must fulfill his moral duty through carrying out the goodness in his heart. So both jen and i were important. In another place, he said he liked life and he also liked i. If he could not keep the two together, he would let life go and choose i.[3] In brief, one should be willing to give up one's life for the cause of righteousness or for the performance of moral obligations. He also emphasized the importance to a ruler of possessing both jen and i. He believed that if the sovereign were jen, all would be jen. If the sovereign were i, all would be i.[4] The influence of the ruler's example or leadership was great.

At greater length than Confucius, he prescribed for rulers what they should and should not do. He believed that a benevolent ruler should bring the people three things: peace, economic security, and education (the second of which had not been specifically discussed by Confucius). In order to preserve peace, a benevolent ruler should not launch wars for territorial expansion or personal ambition of any kind. In case of a just war, a benevolent ruler would find the morale of his army high. He could expect the people of the state with which he was at war to submit to him voluntarily rather than support a ruler of their own who oppressed them.[5] Victory is determined by the virtue of the ruler rather than by his armament.

The second thing a ruler must provide for the people was economic security. He must enable them to have sufficient food, clothing, and shelter. To this end, he should return to the ancient "well-field" system of land distribution and taxation. In this system, a sizable square of land was to be divided into nine equal plots like the Chinese character 井 (which means well from which underground water is drawn). The eight plots surrounding the center plot would be given by the state to eight families. Each family would till its plot and live on the produce of the plot. All eight families would cultivate the center plot and offer its produce to the government as taxation.[6] In this way, the eight families would learn how to cooperate and taxation would be reasonable.

Education was to come after the people were sufficiently fed, clothed, and sheltered. Mencius favored a system of public schools which concentrated on moral education,[7] but he did not give any detailed statement about the organization and curriculum of such schools.

By and large, Mencius put greater emphasis than Confucius on following the best traditions of antiquity. Both Mencius and Confucius believed that a king should be virtuous, but Mencius made this specific by saying that a benevolent king must model himself after the sage-kings of Yao and Shun.[8]

He not only emphasized Confucius' teaching that in government the people, rather than the ruler, should come first; he also defended the people's right to revolt if the ruler neglected his responsibility toward the people or oppressed them in any way.[9]

Mencius stressed the value of the feeling of shame, saying, ". . . [T]he feeling of shame and dislike is essential to man. . . . The feeling of shame and dislike is the principle of righteousness."[10] And again: "A man may not be without shame. When one is ashamed of having been without shame, he will afterwards not have occasion to be shamed (or occasion for shameful conduct)."[11] These sayings seem to have influenced Chinese society to make shame a strong social sanction, comparable to the Western religious sanction of guilt.

Mencius' explanation of human nature differs from what had been asserted by Confucius. Confucius thought human beings were capable of being good. Mencius believed that the tendency of human nature to do good was like the tendency of water to flow downwards. Men could be made to do what was not good just as water could be forced to move upwards.[12] In other words, men were led to evil ways through neglect and abuse of their innate goodness. For this, the environment should be blamed.

## The Life of Hsün Tzu

Hsün Tzu, a native of the feudal state of Chao, lived at the very end of the Chou period. The dates of his birth and death are uncertain, but it has been accepted by most scholars that he was at his prime between 298 and 238 B.C. He was a high official, first in the feudal state of Ch'i and then in that of Ch'u. During the latter part of his life he spent much of his time in writing and teaching.

## Basic Teachings of Hsün Tzu

Hsün Tzu adopted all the basic ethical and political teachings of Confucius. He disagreed, however, with both Confucius and Mencius on human nature and openly critized Mencius' opinion.[13] Hsün Tzu believed that human nature was evil. Whereas Mencius taught that evil was the effect of abuse or neglect of the innate goodness of man and that moral education was the process of restoring that goodness, Hsün Tzu regarded the educational process as the means for altering the original evil propensity of man and encouraging him to seek goodness.

Hsün Tzu believed that man was born with the love of gain and with feelings of envy and hate. If he indulged these, they would lead him into wrangling and strife, violence and crime. Consequently, man must be transformed by the instructions of a qualified teacher and guided by li or the rules of proper conduct established by the sages. In ancient times the sage-kings, realizing that man's nature was evil, not only produced the rules of proper conduct to transform it, but also established the authority of the ruler to control it, set up laws and standards to correct it, and instituted strict punishments to restrain it. As a result, all the world achieved order and conformed to goodness.[14]

In short, Hsün Tzu believed that the best way to direct man from original evil to an acquired good was to enforce strictly all that was prescribed by the ancient sage-kings. He emphasized learning from antiquity even more than Mencius, and allowed no room for the change of times or circumstances. His authoritarian branch of Confucianism diverted the flexible thought of Confucius into sterility and regimentation.

Hsün Tzu's theory of the triad led him to depart from Confucius' concept of Heaven. In his theory, Heaven, earth, and man form the triad. Heaven provides its seasons; earth, its resources; and man, his government. Heaven, which operates with constant regularity, prevails in the same way whether there be a sage-king like Yao or a tyrant like Chieh. Respond to it with good government, and good fortune will result; respond to it with misgovernment, and misfortune will result. Man should do his best under a good government rather than put his hopes in the assistance of Heaven and earth. Since Heaven has its own course, it does not change because of man's prayers.[15] In using this explanation, Hsün Tzu probably aimed at the elimination of the superstitious, contemporary belief in magic, omens, and portents, which hindered human progress. At the same time, he practically equated Heaven with the order of Nature, an opinion quite apart from Confucius' concept of Heaven as the Almighty guiding Providence which controls human destiny. As pointed out by Professor Chan, Hsün Tzu's concept of Heaven as Nature is obviously closer to the Tao of the Taoists than to the purposive Heaven of Confucius and Mencius.[16]

The influence of the thought of Hsün Tzu was greatest during the period of Han (202 B.C.-A.D. 220). It then declined. By the periods of T'ang (618-906) and Sung (960-1279), the thought of Mencius had become the orthodox embodiment of Confucianism.

**Notes**

1. *The Analects of Confucius* is a record of Confucius' conversations and activities probably compiled by the students of his students. *The Mencius* (also translated as *The Works of Mencius*), *The Great Learning,* and *The Mean* (also translated as *The Doctrine of the Mean*) are the best-known works of his followers. These four are called *The Four Books. The Mencius* was probably the work of Mencius' students. *The Great Learning* is said to have been written by Tzu Ssu, Confucius' grandson, or Tseng Tzu, Confucius' student, or by one of the students of Tseng Tzu. *The Mean* was largely written by Tzu Ssu. *The Great Learning* may be called a summary of the Confucian moral, educational, and political program with jen as its center. *The Mean* develops Confucius' moral idea of moderation and balance into a basic norm of human conduct. According to the author the application of such a norm would bring man into harmony with the universe, a metaphysical aspect which was not discussed by Confucius.

2. James Legge (trans.), *The Chinese Classics,* vol. 2: *The Works of Mencius* (London: Oxford University Press, 1895), Book 6, Part 1, chap. 11.

3. Ibid., Bk. 6, Pt. 1, ch. 10.

4. Ibid., Bk. 4, Pt. 2, ch. 5.

5. Ibid., Bk. 1, Pt. 1, chs. 5 and 6 and Bk. 2, Pt. 2, ch. 1.

6. Ibid., Bk. 3, Pt. 1, ch. 3.

7. Ibid., Bk. 1, Pt. 1, ch. 7 and Bk. 3, Pt. 1, ch. 3.

8. Ibid., Bk. 4, Pt. 1, ch. 1.

9. Ibid., Bk. 1, Pt. 2, ch. 8.

10. Ibid., Bk. 2, Pt. 1, ch. 6.

11. Ibid., Bk. 7, Pt. 1, ch. 6.

12. Ibid., Bk. 6, Pt. 1, ch. 2. In ibid., Bk. 6, Pt. 1, ch. 6 he further mentioned that jen (love), i (righteousness), and other virtues were inherent in human nature. If some people had these virtues to a much greater degree than others, it was because those others had not developed their original capability to the fullest extent. Again the blame was put on the environment.

It has been said that Mencius' mother moved three times during his childhood in search of a better environment. That Mencius emphasized environment so much might be to some extent the influence of his mother.

13. Hsün Tzu, *Hsün Tzu: Basic Writings* (Burton Watson, trans.) (New York: Columbia University Press, 1963), sec. 23, pp. 158-59.

14. Ibid., sec. 23, pp. 157-71.

15. Ibid., sec. 17, pp. 79-88.

16. Wing-tsit Chan (trans. and comp.), *A Source Book in Chinese Philosophy* (Princeton, New Jersey: Princeton University Press, 1963), p. 117.

# 6

# The Legalists: Shang Yang, Han Fei, and Li Ssu

*L*egalist school is the literal translation of *Fa-chia,* a Chinese term that has no equivalent in the West. Legalism, or the thought of the Legalist school, therefore, should not be associated with jurisprudence.[1]

Strictly speaking, it is improper to use the term Legalist school. The doctrine called Legalism has no recognized founder. Han Fei or Han Fei Tzu (Master Han Fei), who is considered the greatest Legalist of all, was not its originator, for others who lived before him had been called Legalists. Shang Yang, for example, preceded Han Fei by about a century.

Since there is no English equivalent for Fa-chia, the basic ideas of Legalism must be defined before any account is given of those who taught and practiced it.

Legalism was the antithesis of Confucianism. It rejected the idea of government for the well-being of the people. The people were supposed to exist for the aggrandizement of the state. For the state's benefit, the people were compelled to live, work, think, and on occasion die just as the ruler or government directed them to. A comprehensive set of harsh laws, framed by authority without any participation of the people or safeguards for their protection, was used to enforce compliance. Aggressive warfare was to be used as an instrument to strengthen the ruler's power, to enlarge the state, and to discipline the people.

Unlike the philosophers of other ancient schools of thought, the Legalists made no appeal to tradition. They did not look back to the legendary sage-kings as examples to follow. They believed that a ruler's virtue and wisdom were of no account; his power and position mattered most in government. It was important to look to the present, to be aware of changing circumstances, and to map out programs accordingly. It was also important for the ruler to possess the art of conducting affairs and handling men so that his programs could be well enforced by law.

These Legalist ideas existed as early as the seventh century B.C.,[2] but they were not fully developed as a doctrine until the third century B.C. by Han Fei. Among the Legalists who lived before Han Fei, Shang Yang was the most outstanding; but *The Book of Lord Shang,* traditionally attributed to him, is not regarded by modern scholars as authentic. Consequently, to illustrate the earlier practice of Legalism, only the life of Shang Yang will be presented, not the theory behind the practice (which might not be completely his). Both the life and doctrine of Han Fei and the life of Li Ssu, a Legalist practitioner, will tell how Legalism reached its climax.

## The Life of Shang Yang (d. 338 B.C.)

Shang Yang, as minister of the feudal state of Ch'in, instituted sweeping "reforms" in that state. He reduced the power of the aristocratic families and created a new hierarchy of men distinguished by military merit. He adopted a set of harsh laws to make the people submissive. He caused the people to be organized in groups of families to spy on each other and to be responsible for each other's behavior. Those who reported the guilty to the government were generously rewarded with gold; those who failed to do so were punished by death. Weights and measures were standardized. The people were compelled either to till the land or to weave. Those who produced a large quantity of grain or silk were exempted from forced labor. Those who were too lazy to work were made slaves. Any family with two adult males was forced to divide the family or pay double taxes. As a result of his reforms, the state became rich and its armies strong. He is said to have laid the foundation for future expansion of Ch'in from a state to an empire. Nevertheless, he lost his position as minister because of his involvement in an intrigue. In 338 B.C. he was killed in battle.

## The Life of Han Fei (d. 233 B.C.)

Han Fei was a prince of the ruling family of the feudal state of Han. Both he and Li Ssu of the feudal state of Ch'in studied with the Confucian Hsün Tzu. Both became Legalists later in their lives. In view of the weakness of his family's state, Han Fei tried very hard to persuade its ruler to adopt his reform program for strengthening the state. Failing in this, he became frustrated and put his ideas in writing. Two of his essays came to the notice of the ruler of Ch'in, who much admired them. In 233 B.C., Han Fei was sent to Ch'in as an envoy of Han. The ruler of Ch'in, well impressed by his personality, was about to offer him a government post, but Li Ssu, who had already become a minister of Ch'in, talked the ruler out of it. He pointed out that Ch'in must conquer Han in order to be strong and that Han Fei of the ruling family of Han could not be expected to switch his loyalty to Ch'in. Through further intrigue Li Ssu had Han Fei sent to prison and caused him to commit suicide in 233 B.C.[3] *The Han Fei Tzu*, attributed to him, is the synthesis of his ideas and those suggested by earlier Legalists. He is thus called the perfector of Legalism.[4]

## The Doctrines of Han Fei

Han Fei believed that, in order to govern properly, a ruler must possess three things: power, statecraft, and laws. Each of the three had been stressed as essential by different groups of earlier Legalists, but Han Fei regarded all three as equally important.

To him, power was the means for gaining supremacy over the masses. Only when the intelligent ruler had power could he make use of men according to his statecraft and enforce his laws without resistance.[5]

Statecraft was the art of conducting affairs and handling men; it was what enabled the ruler to keep himself in power. The enlightened ruler appointed officials according to their ability and handed out titles and stipends according to their merits.[6] He would hold his ministers responsible for the office assigned them and control them by means of "two handles," namely, punishment and favor. Punishment meant the infliction of mutilation and death. Favor meant the bestowal of honor and reward. The right of inflicting punishment and bestowing favor was to be reserved to the ruler alone. Once he delegated it to somebody else, he made it possible for that person to overpower him.[7]

Han Fei believed that the only reason the ministers did not assassinate their sovereign was because their parties and cliques were not strong enough. So if the ruler broke up their parties and cliques, it would be like pruning trees in time to prevent their branches from growing larger than the trunk and hurting it. The ruler must have absolute power and wield it like lightning and thunder.[8]

The ruler must always be cautious. He must watch out for intrigues by his ministers, such as the use of beautiful women and servants to delude him. He must be alert to the efforts of his elders and kinfolk to deceive him, of fluent speakers to sway him, and of the neighboring states, especially the larger and stronger ones, to intimidate him.[9]

The laws must be made by the ruler. They must be uniform and inflexible. They must be published so that the people would know what to expect in case either of violation or compliance. They must be enforced by the ministers in the name of the ruler with complete regularity and impartiality. Those who obeyed the law were to be rewarded generously; those who violated it were to be punished severely. The effect of this would be to encourage what was beneficial to the strength and well-being of the state on the one hand and to restrain or prevent evil on the other.[10]

"Therefore, in the state of an enlightened ruler there are no books written on bamboo slips; law supplies the only instruction. There are no sermons on the former kings; the officials serve as the only teachers."[11]

### The Life of Li Ssu (d. 208 B.C.)

Li Ssu, the Confucian Hsun Tzu's student who turned to Legalism, was not a theorist like his schoolmate Han Fei, but a successful politician who put Legalism in practice. On the foundation laid by Shang Yang, Li Ssu, minister of the feudal state of Ch'in, centralized the power of the state, regimented the people, and through aggressive warfare made Ch'in the strongest feudal state. Eventually, Ch'in conquered its last rival, the feudal state of Ch'u. Under the able leadership of King Ch'eng, China was unified and became an empire, the Empire of Ch'in. In 221 B.C. King Ch'eng assumed the title of "Ch'in Shih-huang-ti," or the First Emperor of Ch'in. Li Ssu was made prime minister.

Sweeping changes took place under the new administration. In order to prevent rebellion, all feudal ranks and privileges were abolished and all private individuals were disarmed. To promote effective control of the empire, a strong centralized government was created with the First Emperor at the summit as the absolute monarch. The empire was divided into military areas each with a military governor, a civil administrator, and a supervisory official; each of these was appointed by the central government. Weights, measures, and writing scripts were standardized. Coinage and basic agricultural products were monopolized by the state. In order to improve defense and transportation, public works, including the Great Walls, canals, and roads, were either newly constructed or improved by use of forced labor. Great masses of people were forcibly transferred to new areas and resettled. The frontiers of China were expanded and neighboring peoples were subdued through warfare. Frontier military service and heavy taxation were imposed on the people. The laws were harsh and rigidly enforced. Capital punishment was frequent and all offenses received excessive sentences. Concurrently, generous rewards were offered to encourage the people to do what was beneficial to the state.

This totalitarian system of government led to opposition from men representing schools of thought other than Legalism. Confucian scholars were especially critical of the government. So Li Ssu sent a memorial to the Emperor[12] and succeeded in dealing with the situation in the Legalist way. All literature, other than the history of Ch'in and books on medicine, pharmacy, divination, agriculture, and arboriculture, were ordered to be surrendered from private hands and burned. Those who refused to comply or who criticized the government were put to death. Those who delayed in carrying out the orders were sentenced to hard labor. In 212 B.C. hundreds of scholars were executed or exiled on the charge that they had criticized the government. Many Confucianists who insisted on saying that the government was wrong were buried alive.

The First Emperor died in 210 B.C. after ruling for about eleven years. His son, who succeeded him, was weak and incompetent, so Prime Minister Li Ssu and the powerful eunuch Chao Kao seized power and made the second emperor a puppet. The two men then struggled for first place. In 208 B.C. Chao destroyed Li and also Li's family.

Li's death was soon followed by the outbreak of popular revolts. The second emperor committed suicide and Chao Kao was murdered. In 207 B.C. the Ch'in dynasty came to its end.

The growth of Legalism reflected the changes brought about by time. The feudal system of the Chou kingdom functioned well during Early Chou (1027-771 B.C.) when the king actually ruled. After that, the system gradually declined. As the king steadily lost control, rulers of feudal states within the kingdom fought among themselves. Stronger states swallowed up weaker ones and the struggle for hegemony became sharper and sharper. During Late Chou (473-256 B.C.), power politics largely prevailed and there was little room left for the rulers to practice Confucianism. Legalism thus flourished.

The practice of Legalism led to the expansion of the state of Ch'in into the empire of Ch'in in 221 B.C.—the first time in history that the Chinese people were unified under a central government. Thereafter, the whole region became known to the West as "China." Though short-lived, the mighty Empire of Ch'in left to the Chinese people a sense of unity that had never existed before. In the history of China, however, its reputation was not good. The First Emperor and his Legalist advisers became symbols of tyranny and oppression long condemned by later generations.

Legalism failed to stamp out rival schools of thought, especially Confucianism. Although some of the Legalist methods were used by later rulers, Legalism never became as influential again as it was during the period of Ch'in.

## Notes

1. Yu-lan Fung, *A Short History of Chinese Philosophy* (Derk Bodde, ed.) (New York, 1948), p. 157.

2. Kuan Chung (d. 645 B.C.), prime minister of the feudal state of Ch'i, was among the earlier men who produced Legalist ideas.

3. For details on his death, see *Han Fei Tzu: Basic Writings* (Burton Watson, trans.) (New York: Columbia University Press, 1964), p. 3.

4. Ibid., p. 4.

5. Yu-lan Fung, *A History of Chinese Philosophy*, vol. 1 (Derk Bodde, trans.) (Princeton, New Jersey: Princeton University Press, 1952), pp. 320-21.

6. *Han Fei Tzu: Basic Writings*, pp. 47-48.

7. Ibid., pp. 30-31.

8. Ibid., pp. 40-42.

9. Ibid., pp. 43-46.

10. Ibid., pp. 21-29.

11. Ibid., p. 111.

12. See "Memorial on the Burning of Books" as translated in *Sources of Chinese Tradition*, vol. 1 (Wm. Theodore de Bary, Wing-tsit Chan, and Burton Watson, comps.) (New York: Columbia University Press, 1964), pp. 140-41.

# 7

# Philosophical Synthesis
# Of the Han

*A* few years of turmoil and anarchy followed the termination of the Ch'in dynasty in 207 B.C. In 202 B.C., Liu Chi (or Liu Pang), a farmer's son who became a military officer and rebel, reunited China as an empire. Liu, later known as Han Kao-tsu (the Great-Great Grandfather of Han), maintained the basic system of government of Ch'in, but replaced its harsh laws with moderate ones. He proclaimed amnesties, freed slaves, remitted taxes, and reduced government expenditures. He practiced the Confucian teaching that the ruler should serve justice and exercise his authority for the well-being of the people. He acted with the advice and consent of his ministers and directed his officials to consult with representatives of the people to learn their wishes. During the reign of his sixth successor, Emperor Wu (r. 140-87 B.C.), Confucianism was officially made the state philosophy of China.

This did not mean that all Han emperors were truly Confucian,[1] but because of the good example set by Kao-tsu, later emperors—Confucian or non-Confucian—strove to appear Confucian. Nor did Han Confucianism represent the original teachings of Confucius. A philosophical synthesis took place during Earlier Han (202 B.C.-A.D. 9). Confucianism of the Hsün Tzu branch was adopted as basic, but elements of Legalism, Taoism, and the then-prevalent "yin-yang" and "five-agents" concepts were grafted onto it.

Han Confucianism is very well illustrated by the philosophy of Tung Chung-shu (ca. 179-104 B.C.), the most prominent Confucian scholar of his time. His life is little known, other than that he was the top scholar examined by Emperor Wu[2] and was appointed chief minister to a prince in 140 B.C. It was largely through his influence that Emperor Wu made Confucianism the state doctrine in 136 B.C.[3]

In his writing, *Ch'un-ch'iu fan-lu* (Luxuriant Gems of the Spring and Autumn Annals), Tung adopted as the basis of his Confucianism the theory of the triad—Heaven, earth, and man—of Hsün Tzu.[4] He placed great emphasis on the obligation of the ruler to serve Heaven, earth, and man. He believed that an enlightened ruler, who has received the Mandate of Heaven,[5] should be "the executor of Heaven."[6] He should observe the will of Heaven and make laws for the people accordingly. Heaven, which gives birth to all creatures, is jen, or love to the highest degree. The ruler, likewise, should love the people and rule them with justice.

The ruler should serve the earth, which provides its resources for man. Following the seasons of Heaven and attending to concerns of the earth—to such matters as plantation, irrigation, land usage, and flood control—he would enable the people to have sufficient clothing and food. Popular morality could not be expected without economic stability.

Tung believed that the ruler should serve man by providing education for the people. He was to be a standard, or good example, for the people and must teach them filial piety, brotherly affection, and other virtues. He must assist their cultivation with appropriate rites and music. When the ruler serves Heaven, earth, and man properly, the people will live in peace and prosperity and, as a result, will be obedient to him.

In Hsün Tzu's belief, as we have seen, human nature is evil. In his writing, Tung modified this by saying that the original nature of man is not actually good but possesses the potentiality for good. "From Heaven the people receive their potentially good nature, and from the king, the education which completes it."[7] Tung, unlike Hsün Tzu, who placed his trust in qualified teachers, made the ruler alone the arbiter on matters of education of the people. In this way, he emphasized the responsibility of the ruler on the one hand and made the ruler more authoritarian on the other.

Like other Han Confucianists, Tung accepted the Legalistic idea of empire and the centralized government structure and administration of Ch'in as being necessary for unifying China. Under a ruler like Kao-tsu, the humane and able founder of Han, harmony was achieved between Heaven, earth, and man, and the empire was well governed. However, under the dynastic concept of hereditary succession, it was not to be expected that all emperors could be as Confucian as Kao-tsu. So there was room for the Taoist "nonaction." Tung wrote that the ruler should imitate Heaven. "Heaven holds its place on high and sends down its blessings, hides its form and shows forth its light."[8] If the ruler provides inspiration and employs worthy men to conduct the affairs of government, he can remain exalted and also enjoy success. "He sits upon the throne of nonaction and rides upon the perfection of his officials."[9] His ministers, who were expected to be Confucianists, would effect what was proper.

Tung further applied the concepts of "yin yang" and "five agents" in order both to enhance the position of the ruler and to check him from exercising arbitrary power. Both concepts dated far back to antiquity (their origin is unkown), but they had not become major elements of thought until the Han times. Both were metaphysical and cosmological doctrines.

In the yin-yang concept, the yin and the yang are a pair of opposites. The yang is positive, active, strong, and constructive; the yin is negative, passive, weak, and destructive. The yang connotes male, the sun, fire, heat, Heaven, creation, dominance, spring, and summer; the yin signifies female, the moon, water, cold, earth, nourishment and sustenance, recessiveness, autumn, and winter. The two metaphysical forces of the yin and the yang are supposed to complement each other and so maintain the cosmic harmony. They react constantly to each other on both the metaphysical and physical planes. Each force, as it reaches its extreme, produces its opposite and the two continue to succeed each other in an endless cycle. Their constant reaction was used to explain all processes of growth and change in the natural world.[10]

The concept of the yin and the yang is associated with Confucianism in that it too teaches the "Mean" of Confucius. Since extremes produce opposite reactions, the best thing for man to do is take the middle course between extremes and so keep in harmony with the divine and natural orders.

The concept of the five-agents may be taken as an elaboration of the yin-yang idea. The five agents are the five metaphysical forces of wood, fire, earth, metal, and water. When they are in this sequence, they produce each other. That is to say, wood produces fire (fire which is produced by a wood-drill); fire produces earth (or ashes); earth produces metal; metal produces water (or the deposit of dew); and water produces (promotes the growth of) wood. These five metaphysical forces dominate certain periods of time, usually the seasons in succession. By analogy, a good number of correspondences were derived. For example, wood is assigned to the season of spring, and is associated with the color green and the direction east; fire is assigned to the season of summer, and is associated with the color red and the direction south; metal is assigned to autumn, and is associated with the color white and the direction west; and water is assigned to winter, and is associated with the color black and the direction north. Earth, which is associated with the color yellow, is located in the center and is supposed to help the other four agents in their government of the four seasons. The five agents normally proceed in the order in which they produce each other. They move in a never-ending cycle like the yin and the yang.

The five agents can overcome or conquer each other when they come in the sequence of fire, water, earth, wood, and metal. Water can overcome (or extinguish) fire; earth can overcome (or soak up) water; wood can overcome (or penetrate) earth; metal can overcome (or cut) wood; and fire can overcome (or melt) metal. Changes in human history are regarded as manifestations of these five metaphysical forces. Each dynasty is represented by one force which has its period of rise and decay. Both natural and human events are under the control of that force which happens to be in the ascendancy. When its cycle is finished and it declines, it is followed or conquered by the next force in the sequence which represents another dynasty. This force, in turn, flourishes and has its cycle. So as one force is overcome by another, one dynasty is replaced by another. The course of nature and that of human events interlock.

In his book entitled *Ch'un-ch'iu fan-lu,* Tung explains questions arising out of the activity of the divine, natural, and human worlds through use of the concepts of yin-yang and five-agents. He says:

> The vital forces of Heaven and earth join to form a unity, divide to become the yin and yang, separate into the four seasons, and range themselves into the five agents. . . . The five activities are the five agents. In the order of their succession they give birth to one another, while in a different order they overcome each other. Therefore, in ruling, if one violates this order, there will be chaos, but if one follows it, all will be well governed.11

To follow this order means that the ruler, corresponding to the yang, must serve as the standard or example for the ruled who correspond to the yin. The yang is superior to the yin. Therefore, the ruler, as head of the human world, should justify his superiority through exercising the Confucian virtues of jen or love and i or righteousness as well as exercising wisdom. His high officials, corresponding to the five agents—Minister of Agriculture (wood), Minister of War (fire), Minister of Works (earth), Minister of Interior (metal), and Minister of Justice (water)—must utilize their abilities and fulfill their respective duties with the utmost effort. When the empire is well governed, all phases of human activity will be in harmony with the workings of the divine and natural worlds.

". . . [W]hen an emperor or a king is about to rise, auspicious omens will first appear, and when he is about to perish, unlucky omens will first appear."12 This is because the yang reinforces the yang and the yin reinforces the yin. Things of the same kind activated each other.

Misgovernment in high places calls forth dislocations in the natural world, causing the appearance of comets, drought, locusts, weird animals or birds, and the like. If such omens or portents are not heeded and reform does not come about, calamity and misfortune will result. During the Han period, interpretation of this kind was often used to censure indirectly the emperor and hint to him that changes had to be made in his policy or ways of doing things. As a device, it was in some measure effective.

By and large, Han Confucianism, as advocated by Tung Chung-shu and other Han scholars, succeeded in making the Han rulers authoritarian rather than totalitarian like the Ch'in rulers. Since Tung stressed the superiority of the ruler over the ruled, of the father over the son, and of the husband over the wife, he made the ruler the father, and the husband the exemplar or standard of behavior for the ruled, the son, and the wife respectively.[13] As a result, the authority of the heads of Chinese households as well as that of the head of government was strengthened. The conditional loyalty to the ruler and filial piety to the father as taught by Confucius[14] were increasingly neglected in society. What was generally known as Confucianism departed further from the actual teachings of Confucius.

## Notes

1. Emperor Wu, for example, was more Legalistic than Confucian. He even reverted back to some of the Legalistic practices, such as the enforcement of harsh laws and the emphasis on warfare.

2. For some time during Earlier Han it had been the practice for distinguished scholars, recommended from their home districts, to be examined by the emperor.

3. Wing-tsit Chan (trans. and comp.), *A Source Book in Chinese Philosophy* (Princeton, New Jersey: Princeton University Press, 1969), pp. 271-72.

4. For the theory of the triad, see p. 45.

5. For the theory of the Mandate of Heaven, see pp. 13-14.

6. As translated in Wm. Theodore de Bary, Wing-tsit Chan, and Burton Watson (comps.), *Sources of Chinese Tradition,* vol. 1 (New York: Columbia University Press, 1964), p. 163.

7. Ibid., p. 167.

8. Ibid., p. 158.

9. Ibid., p. 159.

10. The yin-yang concept was also developed by scholars of the Han period in their interpretation of the *Book of Changes,* the ancient book of divination. They expanded the meaning of "changes" into a comprehensive system of cosmology. They equated the trigram of Heaven ☰ with the yang and that of earth ☷ with the yin. Heaven (male) and earth (female) thus became the father and mother of all other trigrams and therefore, of all creation. By their interaction they were held to produce all the phenomena of the world. See p. 14 for the eight trigrams.

11. Translation of Tung Chung-shu in de Bary, Chan, and Watson, *Sources of Chinese Tradition,* p. 202.

12. Wing-tsit Chan, *A Source Book in Chinese Philosophy,* p. 283.

13. Ibid., pp. 277-78.

14. For the conditions set by Confucius, see pp. 24-25. In the *Analects* Confucius never mentions anything about the husband being the standard or exemplar of the wife and that the wife therefore should be obedient to the husband.

# 8

# Neo-Taoism and Buddhism

$A$fter the extinction of the Han dynasty in A.D. 220, the empire split and there was a period of about 370 years of political disunion. During this time the contending states fought frequently among themselves, but none was able to reunify China and build a new empire. The merciless killing in wars, the sharp economic decline, natural disasters such as floods and droughts, and the great political and social instability brought intense suffering to large numbers of people. As classical scholarship lost its vital function in government and society,[1] intellectuals shifted their interest from Confucianism to Taoism. Neo-Taoism, which was an intellectual movement for the revival of Taoism, led to some new interpretations of the old Taoist writings and some slight modifications of the old Taoist concepts. Buddhism, which had not been able to make inroads among intellectuals since its arrival from India during the first century, also developed and gained its foothold during this period of political disunion.

## Neo-Taoism

Neo-Taoism as an intellectual movement took place during the third and fourth centuries. Scholars who participated in this movement, known as Neo-Taoists, centered their efforts on the study and interpretation of *The Lao Tzu* and *The Chuang Tzu*. Many wrote commentaries on these works. The best-known

commentators were Wang Pi (226-249) who wrote on *The Lao
Tzu,* and Kuo Hsiang (d. 312), on *The Chuang Tzu.*

Little is known about either Wang Pi or Kuo Hsiang. Wang
Pi, who also wrote *Commentary on the Book of Changes,* used the
term "nonbeing" (wu) in his *Commentary on the Lao Tzu.* "All
being originated from non-being."[2] In his interpretation, nonbeing is equivalent to "Tao" of *The Lao Tzu.* It refers to ultimate
reality which transcends all distinctions and descriptions and is
always correct, because it is in accord with principle. Whereas
Lao Tzu says things are destined to be so, Wang modified this by
saying that the principles of things make things what they are.
Consequently, small differences of this kind do not change the
basic metaphysical concept of Taoism.

In his *Commentary on the Chuang Tzu,*[3] Kuo Hsiang inter-
prets nonbeing as "a state of nothingness" or what Professor
Fung calls a mathematical zero.[4] Nonbeing or Tao cannot be
regarded as the first cause of things in the world of being. Things
are spontaneously what they are; they are self-produced without
any cause. They exist and transform themselves each according
to its own principle. So Kuo's concept plainly and completely
denies the existence of a Creator.

Both Wang and Kuo upheld in their writings the Taoist
virtues such as nonaction (or taking no unnatural action),
contentment, simplicity, and silence (or quietism). Many times,
however, they used the Taoist philosophy to justify Confucian
behavior and endorse the Confucian virtues. For instance, early
Taoists, especially those who believed in Chuang Tzu, criticized
Confucius for not being able to use reason to control his
emotion over the untimely death of his most brilliant student
Yen Hui. He bewailed his loss with exceeding grief[5] instead of
keeping silence; reason should have told him that death was
simply the natural conclusion of life. Wang, going along with
this criticism at first, argued later that human emotion was
something natural to one's nature. What was natural could not
be changed. Therefore there was nothing wrong with the conduct of Confucius, the Sage, who showed emotion on such an
occasion.[6]

For another instance, Lao Tzu stood for the preservation of
primitive simplicity and therefore the banishment of the accu-

mulated wisdom of the sages. Kuo in his *Commentary on the Chuang Tzu* does not oppose the wisdom of the sages as such, but is against its imitation. Every man, he says in effect, has his own particular nature and particular ability which he should follow and develop. The wisdom of the sages is truly wisdom when it is in accord with what is natural. Whenever it is merely imitated, "love and righteousness straightaway lose their genuineness and propriety and music depart from nature, leaving only their superficial semblance behind."[7] Evidently, love and righteousness and other Confucian virtues were endorsed by Kuo so long as these virtues were genuine.

Unlike Chuang Tzu's sage who withdrew into a hermit's life and contemplated the universe, both Wang and Kuo believed that a sage could remain in the midst of human affairs and make his social and political contribution through taking no unnatural action. He could travel in both the transcendental and the mundane worlds.[8] The Neo-Taoists thus brought forth some compromise between Taoism and Confucianism through philosophical syncretism.

## Buddhism

Buddhism spread to China from India at the beginning of the Christian era. It developed very slowly during the Later Han period (A.D. 25-220), as its teachings were then alien to the Chinese mind. The misery of life during the following period of political disunion probably led more people to put hope in what was beyond the here and now and so Buddhism spread much faster. By the time China was reunited under the Sui dynasty (590-618), Buddhist converts had been made among all classes of people in the empire. The T'ang dynasty (618-906) which succeeded the Sui was known as "Buddha Land."

### Buddha and His Basic Teachings

Buddhism was founded by Siddhartha Gautama, prince of a small Himalayan kingdom of India, who lived about 567-487 B.C. As he grew up, he became disenchanted with the pleasures and luxuries of palace life. He left home and became a mendicant monk. After years of religious striving, he attained "enlightenment." He was then 35 years of age. Known thereafter as the Buddha or the Enlightened One, he preached the message of his new religion until his death at the age of 80. He was also known as Sakyamuni or Sage of the Sakya clan.

The basic teachings of Buddha consist of three main doctrines:

*The Doctrine of Rebirth.* This doctrine, current in the Indian religions of his time, was incorporated by Buddha in his religious system. It says that one lives many lives on earth. The cycle of birth, death, and rebirth may be repeated forever. The life of any individual started from a beginningless past and would extend into the endless future. Whether a person's next life is better or worse than the preceding one depends on the consequences effected by *karma,* which is the Sanskrit word for "deed" or "action."

*The Doctrine of Karma.* Any deed or action performed in one's lifetime bears consequences. This is consonant with the belief of early Hinduism except that Buddha modified it by emphasizing the doer's intention. That is to say, if a deed were performed unintentionally, it would not bear consequences. If an intention were present, the consequences would follow even if the deed were not performed. An automatic settlement of accounts would be made at the time of death. If the good deeds done in a person's lifetime outweighed the bad ones, his next life would be a better one and vice versa.

*The Doctrine of No Permanent Self or Soul.* Early Hinduism believed in the transmigration of a permanent or unchanging self or soul in each individual through successive lives. Buddha did not deny transmigration, but rejected the existence of any permanent self or soul in the individual. His teaching says that the individual is made up of a combination of five components: material body, sensation, perception, psychic disposition, and consciousness. These change every moment, and so the individual is in a state of constant flux. When the individual dies, the combination of five components disintegrates. The immaterial components immediately enter into a new material body. In this new body, the consequences of deeds performed by the individual in his previous life determine the nature of his new life. This is rebirth, but rebirth is not salvation.

Why is rebirth not regarded as salvation? How is salvation

to be achieved? These questions are answered in the "Four Noble Truths" enunciated in Buddha's first sermon. 1) Life at its best means sorrow or suffering, because there must be such things as old age, death, departure from beloved ones, and not getting what one wishes. 2) Sorrow or suffering comes from a craving for sensual pleasures and existence. 3) Sorrow or suffering can be avoided only through the suppression of such a craving. 4) The craving can be suppressed only through moral conduct, mental discipline, and intuitive insight.

Moral conduct means no lying, no killing, no unchastity—no action that is harmful to oneself or to another; it embraces love, compassion, sympathetic joy, and equanimity. Mental discipline starts with the correct effort to control the mind and keep it from craving sensual pleasures or material possessions. It also means training the mind to meditate, and to bring one's thought to bear on one single point and concentrate on it without wavering. When the mind is not disturbed by external elements, it can attain stages of bliss and ecstasy. Intuitive insight presupposes the renouncement of sensual pleasure and the possession of a right view of things, that is, the recognition of the truths that life is sorrowful and impermanent and that there is no permanent self or soul. These presuppositions, together with mental discipline, will enable one to achieve intuitive insight. Intuitive insight will bring one to the state of *Nirvana*.

Nirvana is a state of complete blissful detachment or full enlightenment. It cannot be defined or described in words. One who attains Nirvana is liberated from the endless cycle of birth, death, and rebirth, because in Nirvana there is no ego and so there is nothing to be reborn. Nirvana means salvation.

There are two kinds of Nirvana—Nirvana with residue and Nirvana without residue or final Nirvana. The first is a state of full confidence, tranquility, bliss, and purity. A person may realize it in his lifetime. When he does, he is the happiest person on earth, because he is free from all anxieties or worries. Buddha attained Nirvana with residue at the age of 35. Final Nirvana is the Nirvana attained at death. Buddha, who attained it at the age of 80, said it was profound, indescribable, hard to comprehend, and beyond the sphere of reasoning. He had nothing more to say of it when questioned.

What we have outlined is known as primitive Buddhism or

Theravada Buddhism. It is essentially a discipline for personal salvation—salvation through one's own exertions. Its attainment is difficult and probably cannot be expected without joining an order of monks or nuns. As it developed in India, it was criticized as being too individualistic and even selfish, because it was concerned primarily with individual salvation.

### Mahayana Buddhism

From the first or second century of the Christian era onward, another school of Buddhism arose and developed in India.[9] It was called Mahayana, or the Greater Vehicle (to Salvation). Its followers called the old school (Theravada) Hinayana, or the Lesser Vehicle (to Salvation). There were two major schools existing side by side, but the new school became more popular than the old.

Mahayana offers salvation to all sentient beings. Its doctrine says all sentient beings have the Buddha-nature in them and are therefore capable of being enlightened or saved. Instead of the strenuous discipline of Hinayana, Mahayana teaches that salvation is to be achieved mainly by faith and devotion to the Buddha and love and compassion for all fellow men. Moreover, followers of Mahayana can receive help from a new category of deities called bodhisattvas.

A bodhisattva is generally regarded as a being who is destined to enter final Nirvana because of his own merits, but who delays his final entry in order to remain in the world and help save sentient beings through his love, compassion, and self-sacrifice. He is also believed to be able to transfer some of his own inexhaustible stock of merits to less fortunate beings so that they too can be saved. Faith in the bodhisattva thus makes it easier for many to achieve salvation.

The notion of the Buddha of Mahayana is also different from that of Hinayana. The latter looks upon the Buddha (Sakyamuni or Siddhartha Gautama) as a human teacher who lived on earth, accomplished his mission, and entered into Nirvana. Mahayana regards the Buddha as the eternal being who is the embodiment of universal and cosmic truth and who has many incarnations on earth. Sakyamuni is but one of them.

## The Schools of Chinese Buddhist Philosophy

A number of Hinayana and Mahayana schools arose in China between the fourth century and the seventh century of the Christian era. These schools were founded largely on the teachings of a single Buddhist scripture or a set of Buddhist scriptures; their interpretations of Buddhism varied because of inconsistencies among the scriptures. Many of the Mahayana scriptures contradicted not only the Hinayana sacred writings but one another as well. The Hinayana schools did not last long in China, nor did those Mahayana schools that took extreme positions in their philosophical teachings.[10] Leading Chinese Mahayana schools, which endured and which taught Buddhist philosophy with a distinctive Chinese flavor, included the T'ien-t'ai (Lotus), the Hua-yen (Flower Garland), and the Ch'an (Meditation) schools.

The T'ien-t'ai or Lotus school is distinctively Chinese in its interpretation of the basic Indian scripture—the *Lotus of the Wonderful Law*. The school was founded by the prominent Chinese monk Chih-k'ai (or Chih-i, 538-597) on Mt. T'ien-t'ai in Chekiang province, which is why it adopted T'ien-t'ai as its alternate name.

The basic teaching of T'ien-t'ai is found in the doctrine of the "Perfectly Harmonious Threefold Truth": 1) All things (*dharmas*) are "empty." They are produced through causation and therefore have no nature of their own. 2) Though they are empty, they do enjoy temporary existence as phenomena. 3) The synthesis of emptiness and phenomenal existence is the mean. Emptiness, Temporariness, and the Mean are the Threefold Truth. As the three involve one another, the three are one and the one is three. This mutual identity is the true state of all things in the universe.

The T'ien-t'ai doctrine of the absolute mind further identifies phenomena with the absolute. Absolute mind, it says, embraces the entire universe. All things in the universe depend on this mind for their existence. Absolute mind contains two natures, one pure and the other impure. Its pure nature is responsible for the attributes of the Buddhas, past, present, and future;[11] its impure nature, those of sentient beings and other things in the phenomenal world. Since all phenomenal manifestations are harmoniously integrated in the absolute mind, everything involves everything else. It follows, then, that all sentient beings have the Buddha-nature in them and can be saved. It is the philosophy of One-in-All and All-in-One, the doctrine of universal salvation.

The Hua-yen or Flower Garland school adopted the Indian Flower Garland Scripture as its basic document. As a Buddhist school, it had no counterpart in India. Master Fa-shun (or Tu-shun, 557-640), who first lectured on the Flower Garland Scripture, was the nominal founder of the school. Master Fa-tsang (643-712), who developed the simple ideas of the scripture into an elaborate system, was regarded as its real founder.

The basic teaching of Hua-yen is embodied in the concept of the universal causation of the Realm of *Dharmas*. The Realm of Dharmas, which refers to the entire universe, involves the Realm of Principle, the Realm of Facts, the Realm of Principle and Facts harmonized, and the Realm of All Facts intermingled and mutually identified. Principle is the noumenon; it is static, formless, characterless, and empty. Facts are phenomena or what constitute the phenomenal world. They are dynamic. They have specific forms and characters and constantly transform. Principle and phenomena interact and interpenetrate, and all phenomena are identified with one another. As the result of the interaction and interpenetration of the Realm of Principle and the Realm of Facts, all *dharmas,* or things in the universe, arise simultaneously through reciprocal causation.

Since all phenomena are manifestations of the one unchanging principle or noumenon, they are in perfect harmony with one another. They, as the representations of the same Supreme Mind, are capable of enlightenment or salvation.

In the final analysis the basic teachings of the two schools, T'ien-t'ai and Hua-yen, are rather close, although the detailed explanations of their doctrines are different.

The Ch'an or Meditation school (also known as "Zen" in the Japanese pronunciation when it later spread to Japan) was so named because it attached exclusive importance to meditation.[12] It was founded by Bodhidharma, an Indian prince[13] who came to China during the fifth century and became the first patriarch of the school. *Descent to the Island of Lanka* was the title of the

Indian scripture that he transmitted to Hui-k'e, his Chinese disciple who succeeded him as the second patriarch. This scripture emphasizes the doctrine of inner enlightenment or the intuitive approach to enlightenment. When the doctrine was transmitted to the Sixth Patriarch Hui-neng (638-713), the school split into the Southern School of Sudden Enlightenment and the Northern School of Gradual Enlightenment. The Northern School did not last long. The Southern School, headed by Hui-neng, flourished. Its new doctrine was established by Hui-neng and his disciple Shen-hui (670-762) and it became an essentially Chinese Buddhist school.

Ch'an teaches that the Buddha-nature or Buddha-mind in its highest attributes is present in all sentient beings. Buddha-mind is Emptiness in the sense that it is empty of any specific character. It is inexpressible in words and inconceivable in thought. It can only be apprehended by intuition—directly, completely, and instantly. Intuition is possible only when one can calm his mind and have no conscious thought. Without conscious thought there will be no ego at work and there will be no karma to tie him down to the endless cycle of birth and death and to breed attachment to external objects. To make the mind operate freely, naturally, and spontaneously and so be capable of intuition,[14] conscious efforts such as learning from sacred scriptures, worshipping the images of Buddha, and performing Buddhist rituals, should be dispensed with. In other words, with the exception of meditation all other Indian traditions of Mahayana Buddhism should be abandoned.

Through intuition one may apprehend the Buddha-nature within oneself. When he does, he experiences an enlightenment or awareness of the undifferentiated unity of all existence. He becomes one with the entire universe and perceives how all differences and particulars merge into one fundamental unity. He is in a state of perfect peace; he realizes something that has always been in him but was unrecognized owing to his previous ignorance. This kind of complete and instantaneous enlightenment might be experienced by a person many times in his life.

Ch'an developed into seven sects during the ninth century but was reduced to three sects after the eleventh century. The difference between the sects was largely a matter of the methods used by the different Ch'an masters in teaching their disciples how to realize the goal of enlightenment. The methods used have been of two principal types. In the "lightning" or "shock" type, the master gives illogical or nonsensical answers to the questions of his disciple, shouts at him, scolds him, or even beats him. The purpose of this is to jolt the disciple out of his analytical and conceptual way of thinking and free his natural and spontaneous faculty to intuit. The second method is the method of silent introspection, or sitting in meditation under the guidance of a master. The master here uses verbal instruction in teaching his disciple how to attain tranquility and eventually intuition.

Compared to T'ien-t'ai and Hua-yen, Ch'an, as a school of Chinese Buddhism, has offered little philosophical content that is new. As a religious discipline, however, its methods of practice are typically Chinese. The Indian Mahayana establishes the broad doctrine that the Buddha-nature is in all sentient beings. Ch'an teaches how the Buddha-nature can be apprehended within the person by his own efforts without resorting to externalities such as scriptures and images.

**Notes**

1. The Han practice of selecting Confucian scholars for government positions through civil service examinations in the Confucian classics was suspended.

2. From ch. 1 of Wang's *Commentary on the Lao Tzu* as translated by Professor Chan in Wing-tsit Chan (trans. and comp.), *A Source Book in Chinese Philosophy* (Princeton, New Jersey: Princeton University Press, 1963), p. 321.

3. Kuo Hsiang's *Commentary on the Chuang Tzu* was probably the joint product of Kuo Hsiang and Hsiang Hsiu (ca. 221-300). It has been said that Hsiang Hsiu wrote the *Commentary* but left two chapters unfinished when he died. Kuo plagiarized Hsiang's work, finished the two chapters, and called the entire work his own. See Yu-lan Fung, *A History of Chinese Philosophy*, vol. 2 (Derk Bodde, trans.) (Princeton, New Jersey: Princeton University Press, 1953), p. 206.

4. Ibid., p. 208.

5. *The Analects*, 11: 9.

6. Yu-lan Fung, *A History of Chinese Philosophy*, pp. 187-89.

7. Ibid., p. 219.

8. Wing-tsit Chan, *A Source Book in Chinese Philosophy*, p. 333.

9. Professor Ch'en, unlike most other authors, thinks this school might have developed as early as "during the two centuries immediately preceding the

Christian era." See Kenneth Ch'en, *Buddhism in China: A Historical Survey* (Princeton, New Jersey: Princeton University Press, 1972), p. 15.

10. Examples are the Three-Treatise school which reduced everything to Emptiness and the Consciousness-Only school which reduced everything to Consciousness. For details on these schools, see Wm. Theodore de Bary, Wing-tsit Chan, and Burton Watson (comps.), *Sources of Chinese Tradition,* vol. 1 (New York: Columbia University Press, 1960), pp. 293-309.

11. Since Buddha means "The Enlightened One," the past, present, and future enlightened ones are Buddhas.

12. Since the inception of Buddhism, meditation has been a standard procedure of all Buddhist schools, whether Indian or Chinese.

13. Another saying is that he was a Persian monk.

14. The emphasis on naturalness and spontaneity of the mind and simple way of life reflects the influence of Taoism.

# 9

# Neo-Confucianism and the Reaction Against Neo-Confucianism

*F*ollowing the long period of political disunion, the Sui (590-617) and T'ang (618-906) dynasties reunited China into a powerful centralized empire. At the same time, various schools of Buddhism[1] steadily gained ground and further overshadowed Confucianism. Philosophical Taoism, together with religious Taoism of the masses,[2] also played a role in eclipsing Confucianism. The system of civil service examinations for the recruitment of government officials—initiated by the Han and suspended during the period of political disunion—was resumed and expanded by the dynasties of Sui and T'ang, but the study of Confucian classics for these examinations did little to effect a revival of Confucianism as a living philosophy.

As early as the ninth century, a few Confucian scholars openly deplored the influence of Buddhism and Taoism on Chinese thought. They condemned the Buddhists and Taoists for seeking to escape from the world and refusing to shoulder social responsibilities. They set about to revive the moral teachings of Confucius and Mencius, which dictated active participation in contemporary life in order to build a better world.[3] After the T'ang was succeeded by the Sung dynasty (960-1279), there were many more Confucian scholars who tried to promote a Confucian revival. A number of them expressed new insights about Confucianism in their writings. Chou Tun-yi (1017-1073), for instance, redefined Confucian cosmology and metaphysics. He developed the "Diagram of the Great Ultimate"[4] to illustrate how all beings or phenomena of creation were derived from the Great Ultimate (approximately the equivalent of the Absolute of the West) through the workings of yang and yin and the five agents.[5] Chang Tsai (1021-1077) postulated that the world and all its phenomena were manifestations of a single primal substance which he called ch'i or material-force.[6] Cheng Yi (1033-1107) developed the concept of li or principle as the eternal and unchanging laws that gave identity to the individual objects of creation.[7] Chu Hsi, the most distinguished scholar among them all, synthesized these new insights and basic teachings of Confucius and Mencius into one embracing system, known as Neo-Confucianism.

## Chu Hsi and the School of Principle or Reason

Chu Hsi (1130-1200) was a native of Fukien province in southeastern China. He studied first under his father and later under other scholars. He served the government of the Sung dynasty for some years, but his official life was intermittent and turbulent because of his open criticism of government policies and his strong attacks on wicked but powerful officials. He took an interest in education and agriculture as well as in politics, and spent a good part of his life teaching, studying, writing, talking, and corresponding with the leading scholars of his day. He wrote commentaries on almost all of the Confucian classics. *The Analects, The Mencius,* and two chapters of *The Book of Rites (The Great Learning* and *The Mean)* were selected and grouped by him as *The Four Books.* His commentaries on these books were so well written that they were adopted, along with the texts of *The Four Books,* as the basis of civil service examinations from 1313 to 1905, when the examination system was abolished. Although not much of an original thinker, he demonstrated marked ability in philosophical synthesis. His system of Neo-Confucian thought, based on a combination of the philosophical ideas of his predecessors, was known as the "School of Principle" or Reason.

The School of Principle teaches that the principle of activity and tranquility, deriving from the "Great Ultimate," led to the production of the two metaphysical forces of yang (active) and yin (passive). The transformation of yang and its union with yin brought forth the five agents of wood, fire, earth, metal, and water. Further interfusion of yang and yin and the five agents gave rise to the physical forms of all beings in the universe.

All beings are composed of *li* (principle) and *ch'i* (material-force). Li is the particular principle that makes each being what it is; li is immaterial and unchanging. Each being also holds within itself the Great Ultimate, which is the totality of all principles of all things in the universe.

Ch'i is the material-force or physical substance of the being. It is the concrete manifestation of principle. It is changeable.

The principle as operative in man is his nature, which is good, and which consists of jen (love), i (righteousness), li (propriety), chih (wisdom, meaning especially moral under-standing), and other virtues. Although this nature is the same in all men, the various elements in each individual's material en-dowment are not balanced. Selfish desires, especially, can make one's physical substance impure and obscure true nature. As a result, evils and inequalities arise among men.

In order to reassert his originally good nature, man must do two things. One is the "investigation of things," and the other is "self-cultivation." The "investigation of things" means the study and understanding of the principles of things, including matters of conduct, human relations, and political and social problems.[8] Man's mind is capable of investigation, because it is in essence one with the mind of the universe. Furthermore, man's knowl-edge as derived from the classics and histories, which teach moral lessons and reveal principles of right and wrong, can help him understand why things are what they are.

"Self-cultivation" means the making of a sincere and serious effort to practice the many Confucian virtues—and particularly jen or love—in order to bring a man's conduct into conformity with his nature. By exerting himself over a long period of time, he will overcome his own selfishness, partiality, and other weak-nesses.

Efforts made in the "investigation of things" and "self-cultivation" will enable a man to enter into all things so as to identify himself fully with them and unite himself with the mind of the universe, which is love itself. He will suddenly find everything made clear to him, thus realizing the enlightenment of the sage—that is to say, the Confucian man possessed of both virtue and wisdom.

Evidently, Chu Hsi synthesized the concept of jen (love) of Confucius, the doctrine of jen (love) and i (righteousness) of Mencius, the idea of the investigation of things from *The Great Learning,* the teaching of sincerity in *The Mean,* the yin-yang and five-agents concepts of the Han times, and the new ideas of a number of Neo-Confucian philosophers, including Chou Tunyi, Chang Tsai, and Ch'eng Yi.

Chu's system of thought dominated the later period of the Sung dynasty (1127-1279) and also the Yüan period (1260-1368) when China was ruled by the Mongols. There was another trend of Neo-Confucian thought that originated from Cheng Hao (1032-1085) (brother of Ch'eng Yi) and was elaborated by Lu Hsiang-shan (1139-1192).[9] It existed side by side with that of Chu, but it did not develop into a new school and overshadow Chu's until the Ming period (1368-1644). This new school was the "School of the Mind" or Intuition.

## Wang Yang-ming and the School of the Mind or Intuition

Wang Yang-ming (Wang Shou-jen, 1472-1529), prominent philosopher of the Ming period, was born in a district of Chekiang, the province adjacent to Fukien or Chu Hsi's province. In 1499 he received the highest degree (equivalent to a Western doctorate) awarded under the civil service examinations. He had also studied military strategy. He held a number of civil and military posts until 1506 when he was exiled to southwestern China because he had offended a powerful palace eunuch. While in exile he engaged in meditation and suddenly realized the enlightenment of the sage (or the man of virtue and wisdom).

From 1510 to 1520 he was again assigned to various civil and military posts. Again he had difficulty with his enemies at court, and lived in virtual retirement in his native district between 1521 and 1527, devoting his time to the teaching of his school of thought, known as the "School of the Mind" or Intuition.

Appointed in 1527 to command the suppression of rebellions in Kwangsi, he died in January 1529 on the way back from his successful campaign.

The School of the Mind teaches that man's mind is identical with principle and with nature. Man's mind, in which all things are contained, is one with the mind of the universe. It is originally good; it possesses an innate knowledge of the good. Since it is all-embracing, it is self-sufficient; it does not need to investigate things as advocated by Chu Hsi. Furthermore, if a man should apply his mind to each individual thing and seek the principle in it, this would imply a division between mind and principle which is an impossibility since the two are the same. In his *Instructions for Practical Living* Wang argued that if principles were outside the mind and had to be ascertained by a study of things, then the principle of filial piety and the desire to be filial would no longer exist as soon as parents passed away.[10]

The sage (or man of both virtue and wisdom) has attained an all-pervading unity with existence. The jen or love of his mind enables him to be one with the universe and all things. The ordinary man as well as the sage possesses this unifying quality of love, which exists in the original mind, but in the case of the ordinary man it is obscured by selfish desires. Anybody may become a sage, if he makes a sincere and serious effort to follow his innate knowledge, that is, "the pure intelligence and clear consciousness of the mind."[11] When he makes such an effort, both his thought and conduct will be in conformity with the moral principles of right and wrong. He will be able to suppress his selfish desires and replace them with love. As he returns to the original mind (of love), he returns to the original state of union with the universe and all things. Moral intuition is therefore the way to sagehood.

Wang also developed the doctrine of the "unity of knowledge and conduct." To him, knowledge is the guide of conduct; conduct is the work carried out in the light of knowledge. Knowledge is the beginning of conduct, and conduct, the completion of knowledge. Knowledge and conduct are therefore one and inseparable.

When someone says he knows but cannot do, it means he does not actually know or else his selfishness prevents him from knowing. When the mind is brought to its original state of purity unobscured by selfishness, knowledge is crystallized into the will to act and action naturally follows. In this way, knowledge and conduct are one. Knowledge for Wang, therefore, means "innate or intuitive knowledge." As pointed out by Professor Fung, whether such knowledge actually exists is something that psychology has as yet failed to determine.[12]

Although both schools of Neo-Confucianism emphasized the Confucian virtue of jen or love and of sincere purpose and concrete action in one's conduct, the rationalistic metaphysics of Chu's school and intuitionism of Wang's school had something in common with Taoism and Buddhism.

Wang's teachings as interpreted by his later followers were even further removed from Confucianism. Innate knowledge, for example, was interpreted as something close to conscience with moral implications. It was also interpreted as mystical insight, resembling the intuitive insight of Buddhism. Since Wang for a period of time advocated sitting in meditation, and as his sudden realization of sagehood appeared similar to the instantaneous enlightenment of Ch'an (Zen) Buddhism, his followers of the late Ming period (the late sixteenth and early seventeenth centuries) caused Neo-Confucianism to drift further toward Buddhism, and his School of the Mind was nicknamed the "Wildcat Ch'an School."

## The Reaction against Neo-Confucianism

The corruption of Confucianism by the "Wildcat Ch'an School" and the general moral decline of scholar-officials during the late Ming regime led a number of Confucianists to advocate a needed moral regeneration through a revival of the simple ethical precepts of early Confucianism. Up to the latter part of the seventeenth century when the Ch'ing or Manchu dynasty (1644-1912) had become firmly established, a definite shift in thinking was taking place that gave rise to what came to be known as the "School of Han Learning."

The scholars of this school attacked both schools of Neo-Confucianism. They looked upon metaphysical speculations and literary elegance with scorn. They insisted upon practicality of thought and emphasized inductive research for the broadening of knowledge. They accomplished much in critical study of the ancient literature, exposing forgeries, and reconstituting texts that had long been lost. In their view, the Han commentaries on the Classics were the most reliable—the least contaminated by non-Confucian thoughts. For this reason, their branch of scholarship was called Han Learning.

Following Ku Yen-wu (1613-1682), Yen Yüan (1635-1704), and other early scholars of Han Learning,[13] Tai Chen (1723-1777) emerged as the most prominent leader of the school. Born in a poor family in Anhui province, Tai became a many-sided scholar largely through his own efforts. Most of his life was devoted to scholarly pursuits. He distinguished himself in philology, phonology, historical geography, and mathematical history.

In his *Meng Tzu tsu-i shu-cheng* (Commentary on the Meanings of Terms in the Book of Mencius) he attacked the abstract and transcendental concepts of Neo-Confucianism and rejected the Neo-Confucian idea that the many principles of things were themselves contained in the mind. He believed that li or principle was nothing but the order of things, by which he meant the order of daily affairs such as eating and drinking, and that the mind was simply a physical substance capable of knowing. Neither the Classics nor Confucius or Mencius mentioned that li was the cosmic principle that existed apart from man's feelings and desires and that it should be used to justify repression of man's feelings and desires. Instead of repression, the sages taught that man's desires should be directed along the right way or proper moral path. The truth taught by the sages should be learned from the Han commentaries of the Classics, not the commentaries of Chu Hsi. The Han commentaries were much more authentic, as they were written closest to the times when the Classics were composed.[14] Neo-Confucianism, which was supposed to be a reaction against the influence of Taoism and Buddhism, turned out to be influenced by them. The scholars of Han Learning, therefore, aimed to dispose of Neo-Confucianism and revive the basic teachings of Confucius and Mencius as a living philosophy.

## Notes

1. They covered not only the schools of Chinese Buddhist philosophy which have been discussed in the previous chapter, but also the Mahayana Buddhist schools which had hardly any Chinese philosophical content but were influential among the masses of the people. Among them, the most popular was the *Ching-tu* or "Pure Land" school. This school, which is still influential today, centered on Amitabha (also Amitayus and Amida), the Buddha who is believed to have created the Pure Land (or Western Paradise) out of his boundless love for all sentient beings. Invocation of the name Amitabha is its most common religious practice. Anyone who has deep faith in him and in the Pure Land will be reborn in this paradise and will avoid the endless cycle of birth and death on earth. He presides over the Pure Land and is assisted by Avalokitesvara (known as Kuan-yin or Kuan-shih-yin by the Chinese), the compassionate bodhisattva who is always ready to lead the faithful to salvation. For details on this school, see Kenneth Ch'an, *Buddhism in China: A Historical Survey* (Princeton, New Jersey: Princeton University Press, 1972), pp. 338-50.

2. Side by side with philosophical Taoism was religious Taoism, which began to develop around the first century B.C. as a cult of the masses. Those who practiced it sought immortality on earth through divination, astrology, and magic. Although it was understood that immortality on earth was impossible, an elaborate system of alchemy was developed and practiced to prolong life. The doctrine of living in harmony with nature was also emphasized. As Buddhism spread in China, this cult imitated it in such things as images, temples, a hierarchy of priests, monasticism, and even the belief in heavens and hells. For more details on religious Taoism, see Wm. Theodore de Bary, Wing-tsit Chan, and Burton Watson (comps.), *Sources of Chinese Tradition,* vol. 1 (New York: Columbia University Press, 1964), pp. 256-58.

3. Han Yü (768-824) and Li Ao (fl. 798) are generally regarded as the earliest scholars who advocated the revival of Confucianism. They were forerunners of the Neo-Confucianism that developed in the eleventh century. See Yu-lan Fung, *A History of Chinese Philosophy,* vol. 2 (Derk Bodde, trans.) (Princeton, New Jersey: Princeton University Press, 1953), pp. 408-24 and Wing-tsit Chan (trans. and comp.), *A Source Book in Chinese Philosophy* (Princeton, New Jersey: Princeton University Press, 1963), pp. 450-59.

4. For "Diagram of the Great (Supreme) Ultimate," see Yu-lan Fung, *A History of Chinese Philosophy,* p. 436.

5. For further details, see Wing-tsit Chan, *A Source Book in Chinese Philosophy,* pp. 460-80.

6. For further details, see ibid., pp. 495-517.

7. For further details, see ibid., pp. 544-71.

8. As pointed out by Professor Chan, Chu Hsi, in the investigation of things, "was careful to emphasize equally both the deductive and inductive methods and both objective observation and intuitive understanding." See ibid., p. 591.

9. Ch'eng Hao (1032-1085) emphasized the unity of the human mind with the mind of the universe. He believed that the realization of this unity is jen or love. For details, see ibid., pp. 518-43. Lu Hsiang-shan (1139-1192) elaborated the idea of Ch'eng Hao on the importance of the mind. He declared that mind is identical with principle, with nature, and with the universe. Man's mind is self-sufficient, all-embracing, and originally good. Therefore, man possesses an innate knowledge of the good and an innate ability to do good and does not need to investigate the principles of things. For details, see ibid., pp. 572-87.

10. Wang Yang-ming, *Introductions for Practical Living and Other Neo-Confucian Writings* (Wing-tsit Chan, trans.) (New York: Columbia University Press, 1963), sec. 135, pp. 98-99.

11. Ibid., sec. 244, pp. 209-10.

12. See Yu-lan Fung, *A History of Chinese Philosophy,* p. 605.

13. For their contributions, see H. G. Creel, *Chinese Thought from Confucius to Mao Tse-tung* (New York: New American Library, 1960), pp. 178-84 and de Bary, Chan, and Watson (comps.), *Sources of Chinese Tradition,* pp. 557-60.

14. See important sections of this commentary as translated by Professor Chan in Wing-tsit Chan, *A Source Book in Chinese Philosophy,* pp. 711-22.

# 10

# Sun Yat-sen

*H*ardly any new philosophical theory was developed in China during the last hundred years of the Ch'ing (Manchu) dynasty, when the nation was exposed to Western influence and subjected to extreme Western impact. The Industrial Revolution in Europe during the late eighteenth and early nineteenth centuries brought about the growth of manufacturing first in Great Britain and then in other Western European countries, and created a demand for both markets and raw materials. Increasing wealth created a need for means of investing it. The advance of science and technology had vastly improved transportation and communications; efficient steamships made ocean voyages for trade and/or invasion feasible.

China, complacent in her own cultural achievement and ignorant of the changes that had taken place in the West, was reluctant to abandon her traditional policy of isolation. Efforts of the Manchu regime to stop the British from selling opium to the Chinese resulted in Chinese defeat in wars of 1839-1842 and later years, and in the signing of humiliating treaties with countries of the West. When Japan, long insignificant to the world, became modernized and defeated China in the Sino-Japanese War of 1894-1895, it became clear to the Western countries that China was much weaker than they had believed. This encouraged further European as well as Japanese aggression from 1895 to 1899. The end result was the division of China into "spheres of influence" by various European powers and Japan.

Humiliation at the hands of the countries that had encroached on China and fury over the incompetence and corruption of the Manchu regime, which had shown itself unable to reform or to resist aggression, heightened Chinese nationalism. A revolutionary movement aiming at the overthrow of the foreign (Manchu) ruler and the establishment of a Chinese Republic was supported, especially by young intellectuals and the better-educated elements of society. Under the leadership of Sun Yat-sen, the Revolution of 1911 brought the Manchu dynasty to its end. The Republic of China was created in 1912.

## The Life of Sun Yat-sen

Sun Yat-sen (Sun Wen 1866-1925) was born in a village of the Hsiangshan district of Kwangtung province on November 12, 1866. He was the younger son of a tenant farmer. During his early childhood he studied some of the Chinese classics in his native village. Before he turned thirteen, his elder brother, who had immigrated to Hawaii, brought him there and paid for his education in a school conducted by an Anglican bishop. The teachers of the school were largely British and English was the language of instruction. In a period of about four years he learned basic English and also the basic teachings of Anglicanism. Shortly after he returned to his native village in 1883, he disfigured the images in the local Buddhist temple and enraged the villagers. As a result, he was forced to leave for the British colony of Hongkong where he continued his studies in a Christian mission high school and college. He was baptized a Protestant in 1884. Upon finishing college he made a short visit to Hawaii, then returning to Hongkong he studied Western medicine there and received his medical degree in 1892. He practiced medicine in the Portuguese colony of Macao in 1893 and proved to be a good surgeon,[1] but in less than a year's time he was forced out of practice by the local government probably because of his competition with the Portuguese physicians.

Thereafter he practiced in Canton, the capital city of Kwangtung.

During the years he was in Hongkong he studied the Chinese classics and dynastic histories with a tutor in order to better his Chinese education.² He had been much impressed by the relatively honest and efficient administration of the British colony in contrast to the administration of his native province, which was backward and corrupt.³ From 1890 to 1892 he presented proposals for provincial reform to two progressive officials of Kwangtung, but these proposals got nowhere. In 1894, while practicing in Canton, he sent a petition for national reform in agriculture, education, and law to a high ranking official of the Manchu government in Peking. It was ignored.

The failure of his efforts led him to believe that no reform could come about without revolution, and that the Manchu dynasty must be overthrown. He quit practicing medicine and went to Hawaii, where in November 1894 he organized the Hsing Chung Hui (Prosper China Society). This society, with a membership of over one hundred in 1895, was the source of financial support for his revolutionary activities. The secret oath of the membership included the declaration: "Drive out the Manchus, restore the nation, and establish a republic."⁴

In January 1895 he organized a branch of the Hsing Chung Hui in Hongkong and plotted a revolt in Canton for the overthrow of the Manchu dynasty. This revolt, which took place in October 1895, failed. With a price on his head he escaped first to Hongkong and then to Japan.

The failure did not in any way discourage him, however. In January 1896, he went to Hawaii and spent about six months in fund raising for his revolutionary cause.

An unexpected reunion in Hawaii with Dr. James Cantlie, his former medical professor, made him decide to go to London. After he arrived there on October 1, 1896, the Cantlies found lodgings for him in their neighborhood, which was close to the Chinese Legation. Kidnapped and imprisoned on the third floor of the Legation building on October 11, he was released twelve days later through the efforts of Dr. Cantlie and Dr. Patrick Manson, another former medical professor of his, who brought the matter to the notice of Lord Salisbury, Prime Minister and concurrently Foreign Minister. This kidnapping episode strengthened Sun's self-confidence and sense of dedication.[5] His *Kidnapped in London,* published in England in 1897, spread his name abroad.[6]

Following his release, he resided in London for about two years, making occasional long excursions to the European continent. He spent most of his time in the British Museum Library,[7] reading books on politics, economics, agriculture, military science, and many other subjects. It was probably during this period that he became acquainted with the ideas of Karl Marx and Henry George as well as those of Mill, Montesquieu, and other philosophers.

In 1898 he was in Yokohama, Japan. Between 1903 and 1905 he made his second world tour. He was more successful this time in raising funds from the overseas Chinese and in winning the allegiance of the new intellectuals, the Chinese students in America and Europe.

He was again in Japan in 1905, shortly after Russia was defeated in the Russo-Japanese War of 1904-1905. There the Chinese students gave him a tumultuous welcome, as they believed that his ideas of revolution and Westernization, if realized, could do for China what Japan had achieved.

In the same year he and Huang Hsing, an influential Chinese intellectual living in Japan, organized the T'ung Meng Hui (Revolutionary Alliance). Essentially a secret society, it aimed at the overthrow of the Manchu dynasty. Tokyo was designated its headquarters and Sun was elected its director. The Alliance consisted of some three hundred members who were either Chinese revolutionaries exiled in Japan or progressive Chinese students studying in Japan. In 1906 its membership reached almost one thousand.[8] Later it expanded to include members from other secret societies and progressive students from Christian mission schools in Central and South China, and overseas Chinese in America and Europe. It was responsible for several sporadic outbreaks in China between 1906 and 1909. None succeeded.

Sun was in Denver, Colorado, when the Revolution of October 10, 1911, broke out in the city of Wuch'ang, Central China.[9] After he learned of the revolution from a newspaper, he went to England and to France, where he tried to prevent the execution of loans to the Manchu government.[10] On Christmas Day he arrived in Shanghai, China. On December 29, 1911, the revolutionaries made him Provisional President of the Republic of China which was officially proclaimed on January 1, 1912. On February 13, the day after the Manchu abdication, he offered his resignation. At the same time he recommended that Yüan Shih-k'ai, the man who had been appointed by the Manchu ruler to negotiate terms of abdication, be made Provisional President on three conditions: that Nanking would be the capital; that Yüan would come to Nanking to assume the provisional presidency; and that Yüan would observe the provisional constitution then being drafted. Later the shrewd Yüan retracted his promise, assumed the provisional presidency in his military stronghold of Peking and made Peking the capital of the Republic. It was too late for Sun or any other revolutionary leader to check him.

In August 1912, Sun combined the T'ung Meng Hui with some lesser groups of revolutionaries to form the Kuomintang. This title literally means National People's Party but is generally translated in the West as the Nationalist Party. This new political party attempted to play an important role in Parliament, but failed.

In 1913 when Yüan tried to replace military commanders in Central and South China with men loyal to him, a revolt endorsed by Sun and known as the "Second Revolution" or Summer Revolution broke out in July in the Yangtze valley. In September of the same year it was suppressed by Yüan's troops. The Kuomintang was then dissolved and outlawed by Yüan and Parliament was indefinitely suspended. Sun again fled to Japan. He did not return to Shanghai until May 1916.

Sun spent most of his time in Shanghai writing and lecturing. In the meantime, Yüan failed in his attempt to be emperor and died in June 1916. Although Li Yüan-hung, top military leader of the 1911 Revolution, succeeded as President of the Republic and Parliament was reconvened, the Peking Government was still under the control of the older followers of Yüan. Subsequent to the dissolution of Parliament in June 1917, militarist Chang Hsün tried to restore the Manchu dynasty.

Unable to do anything in the North, Sun went to Canton in July 1917 to lead the Constitution Protection Movement; he established a military government there two months later. This military government was, however, outpowered by the Kwangsi clique; as a result, it was reorganized in April 1918. Once more Sun was obliged to retire to Shanghai and turn his attention to writing.

In October 1920 the Kwangtung army succeeded in retaking Kwangtung from the Kwangsi clique. Sun was invited back to Canton where he resumed the military government in November 1920.

Between November 1920 and August 1922 Sun made a great but fruitless effort to secure financial support from Japan, Germany, Great Britain, and the United States so that he could unify China under a constitutional government. In the meantime, several emissaries from Russia had approached him and hinted at possible Russian support. One of the most significant of these contacts was his meeting with the Comintern agent J. F. M. Sneevliet (pseudonym H. Maring) in Kweilin late in December 1921. In their discussions, the idea for cooperation among the Kuomintang, the Chinese Communist Party (founded in Shanghai in July 1921 under the direction of the Comintern), and Russia was explored.

In 1922 the revolt of Ch'en Chiung-ming, military governor of Kwangtung, forced Sun to take refuge again in Shanghai. Adolph Joffe was sent to Shanghai by the Comintern in January 1923 to carry on talks with Sun. These talks crystalized into the latter's acceptance of three conditions for Soviet aid, namely, to follow the military and political advice of the Soviet Union; to reorganize the Kuomintang; and to admit the Chinese Communist Party members into the Kuomintang as individuals.[11]

The revolt was crushed and Sun was able to reestablish his military government in Canton in October 1923. At this time, Stalin's envoy Mikhail Borodin was sent to Canton to provide guidance for the reorganization of the Kuomintang. The nine-man committee in charge of the reorganization included Ch'en Tu-hsiu, head of the Chinese Communist Party. Although the Communist doctrine was not accepted, the Kuomintang was reorganized along Bolshevik lines. A number of the Chinese Communist Party members were admitted to the Kuomintang as members in 1924, and some of the Chinese Communist leaders became executive officers of the Kuomintang. The Kuomintang-Communist United Front was thus established and it was settled that the two parties should cooperate in a national revolution against imperialism under the advice of the Soviet Union. With Soviet assistance the Kuomintang also established the Whampoa Military Academy in June 1924 in order to train junior officers for the revolutionary movement.

At the invitation of northern militarists who held power in Peking, Sun left Canton for Peking on November 13, 1924. Subsequently he had a number of talks with these militarists regarding national unification and reorganization of the Peking government. Before reaching any agreement with them, he fell ill. He died of cancer in Peking on March 12, 1925.

### Revolution and National Reconstruction

Sun's thought, centering on revolution and national reconstruction, was embodied mainly in his "Three Principles of the People," namely, Nationalism, Democracy, and People's Livelihood. These principles, which were formulated and reformulated between 1894 and 1924, reflected the influence of Western ideas and practices.

His early nationalism—originating in 1894 when the Hsing Chung Hui was organized and reemphasized in 1905 when the T'ung Meng Hui was established—was directed largely against the Manchu regime. Since that regime refused to accept his proposals of reform for strengthening China according to Western models, he believed a revolution was in order. Nationalism, therefore, represented the desire for the overthrow of the Manchu dynasty and the replacement of it with a Chinese republic.

Following the establishment of the Republic of China in 1912, however, he realized that the abdication of the Manchu dynasty had not brought forth the national unity required for a strong state. The Chinese people, like "a heap of loose sand,"[12] needed nationalism to promote cohesion and solidarity. Nationalism thus came to refer to national patriotism, or the transfer of the Chinese traditional loyalties from the family and clan to the state.

After he failed to obtain support from the Western demo-

cratic countries and Japan (1920-1922), he reached agreement
with Joffe in January 1923 for the receipt of Russian aid.
Formation of a Kuomintang-Communist United Front in a
national revolution against imperialism under the advice of the
Soviet Union became his new goal of revolution. The term
"imperialism" was Communist oriented; but unlike Lenin, who
regarded it as the ultimate phase of capitalism, Sun defined it as
"a policy of aggression upon other countries by means of
political force."[13] From then on his nationalism was directed
against foreign aggressors who exercised political and/or economic control over China. He aimed to secure the recovery of
China's lost territories and sovereignty and the attainment of its
independence and equality with other nations.

His second principle of the people was democracy. Theoretically, he adopted Lincoln's "government of the people, by the
people, and for the people" as his own goal. In view of the
difference of background between China and the West he
worked out a democratic system of government for China that
was not entirely Western.

He believed democracy in China should mean a strong
government headed by men of ability with the qualities of
leadership but controlled by the people. Under the basic principle of separation of powers, the Chinese government was to be
composed of five branches—the executive, legislative, and judicial branches originating from the ideas of Montesquieu, and the
examination and control branches patterned after the traditional
Chinese institutions of civil service examination and censor. The
examination branch was to determine the qualifications of members of the five branches of government and of members of the
National Assembly. The control branch was to impeach delin-
quent officials of all branches except its own who would be
impeached by the National Assembly. This five-power constitution was regarded by him as the embodiment of the best
elements of government in the East and West.

While powers of government were vested in the aforesaid
five branches, powers of the people would be exercised through
suffrage, recall, initiative, and referendum. These four powers of
the people were expected to keep a sufficient check on the strong
government.

Sun was aware that after tens of centuries of dynasty rule

the Chinese people were not immediately ready to exercise their powers or rights. So he designed three distinct stages of progress toward democracy. First, upon the overthrow of the Manchu regime there would be a period of military operations for the unification of China. During this period the corruption in officialdom would be eradicated and degenerate customs and superstitions eliminated. The second stage would be a period of political tutelage or guided democracy.[14] During this period, the provisional constitution, defining the rights and duties of citizens as well as the powers and responsibilities of the revolutionary government, would be promulgated. Under the guidance of the Kuomintang the people would be trained to exercise their four powers of democratic self-government in their respective local administrative district known as *hsien*.[15]

The third stage would be the stage of constitutional government. The people, exercising their powers of self-government on the local district level, would elect delegates to form the National Assembly, which would represent them on the national level. Each self-governing district would be entitled to elect one delegate to the National Assembly. It would adopt a written constitution on the basis of which the five-branch Central Government would be responsible to the National Assembly. The people of the various self-governing districts would elect by ballot the President of the Republic who would serve as the chief executive of the state. Sun's democratic system of government was a combination of "direct democracy" and a representative system. It contained elements of Swiss democracy as well as those of the American and British democracies.

His third principle of the people, the "People's Livelihood," was the economic aspect of his program of national reconstruction. It was a moderate form of socialism. Although he regarded Marx as a notable social scientist, he rejected Marx's "class struggle" and "the dictatorship of the proletariat" as inapplicable to China. In Sun's opinion, industry had not as yet developed in China and so there had been hardly any capitalism. The major problem in China was poverty rather than the unequal distribution of wealth. Moreover, even under capitalism the living standards of the working class could rise as American experience had shown.

So far as China was concerned, the problem of poverty

could best be solved by producing wealth without simultaneously creating a great capitalist class. To that end he advocated
the regulation of capital through a kind of state socialism that
was in fact a mixed economy. Major enterprises and utilities,
such as mining, railroad, water ways, postal and telegraph
services, would be nationalized in order to prevent monopoly.
Small-scale enterprises, such as the textile and cement industries,
would be left to private hands. Foreign investment was permitted on the condition that it would not control the Chinese
economy in any way. Foreign economic imperialism on the basis
of "unequal treaties"[16] was to be removed. China was to gain
customs autonomy and erect protective tariffs so that its infant
industries could survive and thrive.

Regulation of capital would have to be accompanied by the
equalization of landownership. A land tax program was needed
under which the government would levy a tax proportionate to
the price of the land and would have the right to buy the land at
its declared price. The price of the land would be fixed by the
landowner. If he undervalued the land, the government would
buy it at the price declared by him. If he overvalued it, he would
have to pay heavy taxes. Since neither would be to his advantage,
he would have to report the true market value to the government. Following the year of assessment, all increases in land
value would revert to the community through the government.
This was because these increases came about through improve-
ments made by society, such as the development of industry and
commerce and the improvement of irrigation.

Sun's socialist ideas were drawn largely from the Fabian
Society and the program of the British Labor Party rather than
directly from Karl Marx. Indeed, his tax program for the equalization of landownership was copied almost entirely from Henry
George's *Progress and Poverty*, published in 1879.

It may therefore be concluded that Sun Yat-sen was a
courageous revolutionary, a frustrated patriot, and a moderate
socialist. His intensive study of Western political and social
theories and his keen observation of events and problems as they
developed in the Western societies enabled him to select those
elements in the Western experience that were most suitable to
China in formulating his political philosophy and program of

national reconstruction. At the same time, being Chinese, he did not completely discard what was Chinese.

Following Sun's death in 1925, the Kuomintang based itself on his thought even more than during his lifetime. Under the leadership of Chiang Kai-shek, the Kuomintang government made it mandatory for all schools to study Sun's Three Principles of the People. All educational institutions and government agencies were obliged to hold a weekly memorial service (every Monday) in which Sun's last will and testament—emphasizing his statement "revolution has not yet been accomplished; comrades must strive on"—was read as the indisputable highest teaching of the land.[17] This kind of indoctrination, however, did not seem to have much influence on the thinking of young people. The spread of Western ideas was largely the effect of the New Culture movement, which will be discussed in the next chapter.

## Notes

1. Dr. James Cantlie, Sun Yat-sen's medical school professor, recognized him as a good surgeon. See James Cantlie and C. Sheridan Jones, *Sun Yat-sen and the Awakening of China* (New York and London: Fleming H. Revell, 1912), p. 31.

2. C. Martin Wilbur, *Sun Yat-sen: Frustrated Patriot* (New York: Columbia University Press, 1976), p. 12.

3. Harold Z. Schiffrin, *Sun Yat-sen and the Origins of the Chinese Revolution* (Berkeley and Los Angeles: University of California Press, 1968), p. 29.

4. Robert Bruce, *Sun Yat-sen* (London: Oxford University Press, 1969), p. 27.

5. Schiffrin, *Sun Yat-sen and the Origins of the Chinese Revolution*, p. 128.

6. Ibid., p. 126.

7. Bruce, *Sun Yat-sen*, pp. 32-33. Schiffrin, however, said that Sun spent the first five months of 1897 reading in the British Museum Library. See Schiffrin, *Sun Yat-sen and the Origins of the Chinese Revolution*, pp. 134-35.

8. Schiffrin, *Sun Yat-sen and the Origins of the Chinese Revolution*, p. 362.

9. This revolution was not previously planned. It started from an accidental bomb explosion in the city of Hankow, Central China, on October 10, 1911 at the headquarters of a revolutionary group where bombs had been secretly made. The police secured lists containing the names of local revolutionaries and a few of them were arrested and executed. For fear of further action, revolutionaries among the troops at Wuch'ang (a city opposite Hankow on the far bank of the Yangtze river) led a mutiny. The troops forced

their commander, Colonel Li Yüan-hung, to assume leadership and the Revolution of 1911 began.

10. Wilbur, *Sun Yat-sen: Frustrated Patriot,* p. 19.

11. It was not a merger of the Chinese Communist Party into the Kuomintang. Individual Chinese Communist Party members admitted to the Kuomintang would have dual party membership. The Chinese Communist Party would not lose its independence as a party, although its members who joined the Kuomintang were supposed to accept the Kuomintang discipline.

12. Sun used this expression in his first lecture on Nationalism, 1924. A passage of this lecture, including this expression, has been translated in Wm. Theodore de Bary, Wing-tsit Chan, and Chester Tan (comps.), *Sources of Chinese Tradition,* vol. 2 (New York: Columbia University Press, 1960), pp. 106-07.

13. Sun Yat-sen, *San Min Chu I* (Three Principles of the People) (Frank W. Price, trans.) (Shanghai, China: Commerical Press, 1928), p. 79.

14. In the *Manifesto of the Military Government of the Revolutionary Brotherhood* made public in 1911, and also in *A Program of National Reconstruction* of 1918, he mentioned that the period of political tutelage would last for six years; but in his *Outline of National Reconstruction* written in 1924 shortly before his death, he did not provide any time schedule for this period.

15. At the time of his writing, there were eighteen provinces in China, subdivided into over 1,500 local administrative districts called *hsien,* each headed by a magistrate.

16. "Unequal treaties" referred principally to those treaties that provided extraterritoriality, mining rights, and leased territories to foreign countries, and foreign control of the Chinese customs.

17. This practice was interrupted in whole or in part during the war of resistance against the Japanese, 1937-1945, and the period of civil war between the Kuomintang and the Communists, 1945-1949. It was resumed after Chiang Kai-shek moved his government to Taiwan in 1949.

# 11

# Leading Proponents of a New Culture: Ch'en Tu-Hsiu and Hu Shih

$C$hinese defeat in wars with Western countries and Japan during the nineteenth century (mentioned previously) made it clear that China must modernize if she was to resist aggression successfully. Shortly after the mid-nineteenth century, a small number of young men were sent to the United States for advanced education. Foreign language institutes, technical schools, and military academies were also established in leading cities of China. The system of civil service examinations on the "Confucian classics" (ancient Chinese classics) was abolished in 1905. More Chinese students were sent to study abroad. A greater number of Western and Westernized instructors were engaged to teach in schools and colleges. By the end of dynasty rule in 1912, secondary and higher education on the Western model had come into existence in all major cities of China. Schools under foreign missionary auspices, established during the 1840s, also increased. As a result, Western ideas, ranging from liberalism to radicalism, gradually influenced Chinese intellectuals and the better educated groups, especially college students. The growth of nationalism, spurred by the "Twenty-One Demands" of Japan of 1915 and the decision in

1919 at the Paris Peace Conference to transfer to Japan pre-World War I special privileges of Germany in Shantung,[1] further heightened the demand for modernization.

Between 1915 and 1923 the "New Culture Movement" took place. This movement, led by Ch'en Tu-hsiu, Hu Shih, and other Chinese intellectuals,[2] aimed at the destruction of what was left of traditional "Confucian culture" and its replacement with what was modern. From 1917 to 1919, intellectuals who had adopted different schools of Western thought discussed and debated how China should be modernized in a ferment of periodical literature. Despite the differences in approach, the great majority of these intellectuals agreed that democracy and science should be the center of a new culture; however, the success of the Bolshevik Revolution of 1917 encouraged some Chinese intellectuals to move toward the radical line and by 1920 there was a split in the New Culture leadership. One branch headed by Ch'en Tu-hsiu shifted to Marxism. The other, led by Hu Shih, maintained its faith in Western democracy.

## The Life of Ch'en Tu-hsiu

Ch'en Tu-hsiu (1879-1942) was a native of Anhwei province. He intensively studied Chinese classics before he traveled and studied in Japan in 1902 and 1906. After he finished the special short courses of Tokyo Higher Normal School, he traveled in France for a period of time. Although not a member of Sun Yat-sen's Revolutionary Alliance,[3] he participated in the Revolution of 1911 and was involved in the Second Revolution of 1913.[4] The failure of the latter forced him to flee to Japan.

He returned to China in 1915 and in Shanghai edited a modern monthly entitled *Ch'ing-nien tse-chih* (The Youth Magazine). Later it was renamed *Hsin ch'ing-nien* (The New Youth). It was very influential among students. In the first issue, dated September 15, 1915, he urged his young readers to maintain a progressive attitude toward change and to adopt a utilitarian approach to new ideas and new techniques. He also encouraged them to understand the world and China's place in it. In the December 1916 issue he attacked Confucianism vehemently as the ethics of a feudal age which had no place in modern times.

Many Chinese customs and abuses, he claimed, that were sanctioned by Confucianism[5] promoted conformism and authoritarianism. In later articles, he advocated abolition of Confucianism in order to make room for individualism, social progress, science, and democracy.

In 1917 he became Dean of the School of Arts at National Peking University, where a faculty of different political persuasions, ranging from conservative to radical, was to be found.[6] From 1917 to 1919 he and Hu Shih, Professor of Philosophy at the same university, led the New Culture Movement along liberal lines. After 1919 he turned steadily toward Marxism or Bolshevism; in several 1920 issues of *The New Youth* he declared his complete faith in Karl Marx. He said that China's social system would have to be changed through class struggle and war, and the inequality and hardship imposed on the workers removed through the abolition of capitalism. Following the overthrow of the capitalists in a class struggle, the creation of a proletarian state in China would be the necessary step. The revolutionary spirit of Russia should be imitated.[7]

It was also in 1920 that he was approached by Grigorii Voitinsky, an agent of the Third Communist International (Comintern), to discuss the organization of a nationwide Chinese Communist Party. This contact led him to invite Li Ta-chao (1888-1927), junior leader of the New Culture movement and Chief Librarian of National Peking University, and other Marxist intellectuals from other parts of China, to meet in Shanghai. There they secretly drew up an organization plan and chose Ch'en Tu-hsiu and Li Ta-chao as the top leaders of the Communist movement in China. Ch'en was responsible for the movement in South China, and Li in North China.

The Chinese Communist Party was formally established in July 1921 with Ch'en as Secretary-General or head of the Party. Following instructions of the Comintern, he directed the Communist movement in China through the period of the Kuomintang-Communist United Front, 1924-1927.[8] The early period of alliance with the Kuomintang brought success to the Communists, since the alliance helped provide the Communists with ready access to the popular movement. The Chinese Communist Party grew speedily, showing its influence in the appearance of militant student and labor organizations, anti-imperialist crusades, and peasant uprisings; however, before it managed to overthrow the Kuomintang, the alliance was terminated in 1927[9] with the purge of Communists from the Kuomintang. Ch'en was held responsible for the Communist setback and was removed from his post. In 1928 he was condemned as a Trotskyite and was subsequently expelled from the Chinese Communist Party.

He was imprisoned by the Kuomintang or Nationalist Government in 1933, but was released four years later when the Kuomintang and the Chinese Communist Party again formed an alliance—the United Front for the Resistance of Japanese Aggression. He died unnoticed in 1942.

## The Life of Hu Shih

Hu Shih (1891-1962) came from a well-known family of scholars in the province of Anhwei; he was born in Shanghai on December 17, 1891. He received a solid Chinese classical education in his early youth. Between 1904 and 1908 he attended three modern private schools in Shanghai where he studied Western history, science, mathematics, and English as well as Chinese. He passed the examinations for the Boxer Indemnity Scholarship[10] in 1910 and went on to take his advanced education in the United States. At first he studied agriculture at Cornell University. Later, realizing that his interest was more in the field of philosophy, he devoted himself to that study and received his B.A. degree from Cornell in 1914. Fascinated by John Dewey's experimentalism, he enrolled as a graduate student at Columbia University in 1915 and in two years' time accomplished his doctoral studies under the guidance of Dewey. He became the leading Chinese advocate of Dewey's thought.

Upon returning from the United States in 1917, he was made Professor of Philosophy of the School of Arts, National Peking University, under the deanship of Ch'en Tu-hsiu. As the leaders of the New Culture Movement, both he and Ch'en declared that Confucian traditionalism must be replaced by complete modernization or Westernization. In his writings on this point, Hu relies on William James's pragmatic concept of truth. Not only do species change as taught by Charles Darwin,

Hu says, truth also changes. It changes with the change of the environment. The Confucian concept of loyalty to the emperor, for instance, was called truth during the dynasty rule. When the Republic of China was established in 1911, the concept lost its function and was therefore no longer the truth. Truth is called truth because of its utility. When a particular truth loses its utility, it is the responsibility of the intellectuals to search for a new truth to take its place.[11]

Believing that the intellectuals should motivate changes in proper sequence and direction according to the demand of the times, Hu motivated literary reform (known as the "literary revolution" because of the great change involved) in 1917. With the support of Ch'en Tu-hsiu he made an assault on the Chinese classical language. He regarded it as a language dominated by Confucian tradition and therefore a dead language in modern times. When modern writers tried to imitate the ancients in the latter's rigid literary form or style, or paid too much attention to tones, rhythm, words, and phrases, they too often produced literary works without substance—without feeling or thought (that is to say insight, knowledge, and ideals) or both. He felt that this was the principal cause of the deterioration of litera-ture.[12] In order to produce a vital living literature the spoken language should be used in writing. Popular expressions and popular forms of Chinese characters, usually regarded by literary men as vulgar, should not be avoided. Writing in the vernacular could serve as an educational tool to popularize new ideas and still possess a literary quality sufficient to justify its existence.

So he wrote everything, prose and poetry alike, in the plain spoken language, creating a style of writing that was both lively and lucid and that appealed to many educated readers. Gradu-ally, the use of the vernacular in writing was accepted as the regular way of writing in schools, colleges, and various academic circles. This success made him known as the father of the "Chinese Renaissance."

Hu was with the National Peking University from 1917 to 1927 as Professor of Philosophy, serving concurrently from 1922 to 1927 as Dean of the College of Arts. He was the President of China National Institute in Shanghai from 1928 to 1930, but returned to the National Peking University as Professor of Philosophy and Dean of the College of Arts from 1930 to 1937. During this twenty-year period he wrote numerous books, articles, and speeches, mainly in the fields of philosophy, history, and politics. Influenced by Thomas Huxley's skepticism, he refused to accept in his writing any beliefs traditionally accepted until he found sufficient evidence to substantiate them. As a follower of John Dewey, he adopted the latter's experimentalist methodology, which he referred to as the scientific methodology of thought. He acknowledged his indebtedness to these two scholars[13] and constantly advocated the importance of first establishing a hypothesis and then seeking evidence for its support as the correct approach to the study of any problem.

Among the writings in which he introduced Western ideas he had much to say about freedom and democracy. Among the different kinds of freedom—freedom of religion, thought, speech, publication, and others—he emphasized especially freedom of thought. In tracing the development of the ancient civilizations of the East and West, he concluded that freedom was the source of all great civilizations. Freedom of thought was particularly important, because every kind of culture product or creation—artistic, scientific, literary, political, and others—derived from it. Freedom left room for nonconformity and encouraged the development of individuality without which no society or nation could improve or grow.

Freedom, equality, and the rule of law were for him the basic elements of democracy. Democratic government meant constitutional government. It required only that a qualified electorate be able to exercise its civic rights properly. He felt it would not be hard to train the Chinese people to exercise such rights.[14] This does not imply that he was unaware of the people's political backwardness, as in an earlier article he had pointed out that ignorance was among the five "enemies" or evils of China,[15] yet he had faith in the ordinary man, in his capacity for self-government, and in his potential as a moral being. Given education, legislation, and constitutional processes of government, he believed the people would make progress toward the practice of democracy.

Because of his emphasis on freedom, he was against all forms of authoritarianism or dictatorship of the right or left. He supported Sun Yat-sen's "Five-Power Constitution,"[16] but criticized Sun for being less inclined to practice democracy following the reorganization of the Kuomintang or Nationalist Party in 1923. He frequently criticized Chiang Kai-shek and his government for being nondemocratic. For example, it became mandatory shortly after Sun's death for government agencies and educational institutions to hold a weekly memorial service at which Sun's last will and testament was read as the supreme teaching of the land. Hu criticized this as an act of absolute authoritarianism that would bring about the loss of freedom of thought. He wrote much also in criticism of Japanese militarism, Italian Fascism, and German Nazism as well as Russian Socialism. Shortly after the establishment of the People's Republic of China in 1949, the Communist regime enforced thought reform, known to the West as "brainwashing." The people were compelled openly to praise Mao Tse-tung's system of thought as the only correct one. Hu remarked that the people had lost not only their freedom of thought but also their freedom to keep silent. This was totalitarianism.

Hu was an independent. He did not affiliate with any political party. However, when he had to take a side during crucial periods, his sympathies were with the Nationalists. He supported Chiang Kai-shek in the war of resistance against Japanese aggression, 1937-1945, and accepted appointment by Chiang as Ambassador to the United States from 1938 to 1942. Between 1943 and 1945, he was in the United States, lecturing at Harvard and Columbia Universities, and serving as a consultant to the Oriental division of the Library of Congress. In 1945 he was appointed a member of the Chinese delegation to the San Francisco conference for the establishment of the United Nations. Later in the same year he headed the Chinese delegation to the UNESCO conference in London. Following the unconditional surrender of Japan in 1945, he became Chancellor of the National Peking University.

Shortly before the establishment of the People's Republic of China in 1949, he left his position and fled to the United States. There he remained for about nine years, working primarily as a scholar and serving for a time as the Curator of the Gest Oriental Collection at Princeton University. He made a brief visit to Taiwan in 1952-1953, and was there again in 1954 to attend the sessions of the National Assembly at which Chiang Kai-shek was elected President of the Republic of China for the second term. In 1958 he accepted Chiang's offer to be the President of Academia Sinica, the highest institution of learning of the Nationalist government.

Between 1938 and 1962 he devoted to writing whatever time he had after fulfilling his official duties. He never changed his political or philosophical stand. As President of the Academia Sinica, 1958-1962, he strove to improve the facilities for scientific education on Taiwan and to promote Sino-American scholarly cooperation. He died of a heart attack on February 24, 1962, after presiding at a reception for newly elected fellows of the Academia.

Hu lived by a philosophy which derived predominantly from John Dewey's thought. He believed in developing one's individuality to the fullest and forging oneself into a finished instrument according to one's talent and capacity in order to be of use to society. Experience is life and life is dealing with environment. In the process of dealing with environment the function of thought is the most important. Thought must be directed by scientific methods, whereby creative intelligence is promoted to solve human problems; only by creative intelligence are produced the new methods and tools required to realize the bright future man may envisage. The individual dies; but his virtue, deeds, and words will leave a permanent imprint on the society of mankind which will never die. Active participation in the improvement of society in order to bring greater happiness to a greater number of people at present and in future is therefore the goal of life. Hu actually lived by this goal. In fact, he lived a life rather close to the basic ethical teaching of Confucius, i.e., to make one's best effort to build a "paradise on earth" for the well-being of the people. When Hu condemned Confucian traditionalism, he meant to eliminate what was out-of-date and those corruptions of Confucianism that had been developed following the great teacher's death.

The philosophy of Hu Shih, reenforced by the way he actually lived, had an influence on many young people. His literary reform also bore fruit. His initiation of writing in the

Chinese spoken language instead of the classical language was comparable to Dante's substitution of Italian for Latin as the way of writing during the Renaissance. Writing in the vernacular in China has succeeded as an educational tool for popularizing new ideas among the general public. Due to Hu's influence, popular works from the early centuries, especially drama of the Yüan period (1260-1368) and fiction of the Ming period (1368-1644), have been rehabilitated as living literature. Whether writing in the vernacular has produced in its own right a contemporary literature of great literary distinction, remains a question for future historians and critics to answer.

The new historical and critical approach to the study of Chinese philosophy and literature which was advocated during the New Culture Movement owed its inception to Hu Shih. His writings, ranging from his *Outline of the History of Chinese Philosophy* (Chung-kuo che-hsüeh shih ta-kang) published in 1919 to his later essays on the study of *Commentary on the Book of Waterways* (Shui-ching chu),[17] reflect his spirit of doubt in the values of antiquity and traditional beliefs unless they could be substantiated by sufficient evidence or proof for which he laboriously searched. The experimentalist methodology of the West, applied by him and other Chinese scholars, thus took root in China.

Like Voltaire in the European period of Enlightenment, Hu might be called the strongest publicist of freedom and democracy in twentieth-century China. The influence of his thought on mainland China, especially in the National Peking University, was so great that the Chinese Communist regime had to stage a vigorous nationwide campaign in 1955 to root it out. Eight volumes of *Criticisms of the Thought of Hu Shih* (Hu Shih ssu-hsiang p'i-p'an) were published for this purpose. He was condemned as "the servant of imperialistic interests,"[18] but people on the island of Taiwan admired him and respected him. While he was living, many young people wrote and asked him to have his writings reprinted in order to replace copies that had been lost or worn out.[19] More recent writings of his, which had never been published, were collected and published shortly after his death. Many Taiwan scholars have analyzed his writings and published books and articles to praise him and to spread his thought further. He has been referred to as "the leading mentor of freedom" and "the fighter for democracy."[20]

### Notes

1. The Twenty-One Demands of Japan of 1915 were divided into five groups. If completely accepted, they would have rendered all China a Japanese sphere of influence. Following a period of negotiation of almost five months in 1915, President Yüan Shih-k'ai accepted the first four groups, which called for Japanese control of Shantung, Manchuria, Inner Mongolia, the southeast coast of China, and the Yangtze valley. The fifth group, which was held in reserve, demanded employment of Japanese advisers in Chinese political, financial, military, and police administrations; and the purchase of at least 50 per cent of China's munitions from Japan.

The Paris Peace Conference of 1919 yielded to the Japanese demand that Shantung, Germany's sphere of influence in China, be shifted to Japan, as Japan had been on the side of the Allied Powers that defeated Germany. The Conference accepted this demand despite the protest of the Chinese delegation, which pointed out that China, too, had been on the side of the Allied Powers.

2. They included Chancellor T'sai Yü-p'ei of National Peking University, Chief Librarian Li Ta-chao of the same university, prominent writers Lu Hsün and Chou Tso-jen, and other professors and writers.

3. See p. 84 for a discussion of Sun Yat-sen's Revolutionary Alliance.

4. See pp. 84-85 on the Revolution of 1911 and the Second Revolution of 1913.

5. Here he meant Confucianism as practiced in common life rather than Confucianism as originally taught by Confucius. Although exaggerated, his claim was not completely groundless. In common life, a person in a superior position many times took the teachings of Confucius out of context and imposed injustice on a person of inferior position. A father could constantly make unreasonable demands on his son by saying that it was the teaching of Confucius that the son should be obedient to his father. A good-for-nothing younger brother who was spoiled and defended by a parent or parents could live on the efforts of an older brother who was hard working. This perversion of the teachings of Confucius was referred to by many as Confucianism.

6. This was made possible by Chancellor Ts'ai Yüan-p'ei who broke the conservative tradition of National Peking University and advocated academic freedom.

7. For further details, see *Hsin Ch'ing-nien* (The New Youth), 8: 1 (1920), 3-11. This article was later reprinted in *Tu-hsiu wen-ts'un* (Collected Essays on Ch'en Tu-hsiu), four vols. (Shanghai: Ya-tung Bookstore, 1927), vol. 3, book 2, pp. 93-100.

8. See pp. 86-87 for more information on the United Front.

9. In April 1927, Chiang Kai-shek made a surprise attack on the Communists that led to a massacre of Communist-organized workers in Nanking, Shanghai, and Canton. In July 1927, all Communists were purged from the Kuomintang. The Kuomintang-Communist United Front thus came to its end.

10. The Boxer Indemnity Scholarship was financed by funds remitted to the Chinese government by the United States from its share of the Boxer Indemnity of 1901.

11. Hu Shih, *Hu Shih wen-ts'un* (HSWT) (Collections of the Essays of Hu Shih), four collections (Taipeh, Taiwan: The Far East Book Company, 1953) (reprinted), col. 1, vol. 2, pp. 309-10. This essay was first published in *Hsin ch'ing-nien* (The New Youth), 6:4 (April 1919).

12. For a more detailed discussion of literary reform, see HSWT, col. 1, vol. 1, pp. 5-17. It was published first in *Hsin ch'ing-nien* (The New Youth), 2:5 (January 1917).

13. HSWT, col. 4, vol. 2, p. 608.

14. *Tu-li p'ing-lun* (The Independent Critic), 130 (1934).

15. HSWT, col. 4, vol. 2, pp. 431-35.

16. Sun's Five-Power Constitution, which was discussed previously, was his constitutional scheme. This scheme was later adopted by Chiang Kai-shek. It consisted of the legislative, executive, and judicial branches comparable to those of the West and the branches of examination and control that were traditionally Chinese.

17. It is a sixth-century work on geography edited by a number of scholars of later centuries. Hu made a critical study of its different editions. He pointed out the defects of certain editions and disclosed forgeries.

18. For a full range of Communist criticism of Hu, see *Hu Shih ssu-hsiang p'i-p'an* (Criticisms of the Thought of Hu Shih), eight volumes (Peking: San-lien Bookstore, 1955).

19. See Hu Shih's Preface of *Hu Shih wen-ts'un.*

20. Yang Ch'eng-pin, *Hu Shih ti cheng-chih ssu-hsiang* (The Political Thought of Hu Shih) (Taipeh, Taiwan: Commercial Press, 1967), p. 167.

# 12

# Mao Tse-tung

$M$ao Tse-tung was prominent as early as the inception of the Chinese Communist Party in 1921, but it took him a long time to emerge as the top leader of the Party. Ch'ü Ch'iu-pai became head of the Party after the first Party leader Ch'en Tu-hsiu was deposed in 1927. Ch'ü, Moscow correspondent for the *Peking Morning Post* in 1920, and later Chinese Communist Party representative in the Communist International or Third International (Comintern), directed a series of uprisings in the latter part of 1927 whose failure led to his ouster in 1928. His successor Li Li-san, who was educated in France and established the Paris branch of the Chinese Communist Party in 1921, had the support of both the U.S.S.R. and the Comintern. In 1930, however, he too was ousted because of his failure in leading urban insurrections.

Between 1931 and 1936 those who had control of the Chinese Communist Party were returned students from Europe. Known as "International Communists," they, under the instruction and guidance of the Comintern, followed the conventional Marxist-Leninist theory and practice of making the proletariat or working class "the vanguard of revolution." They organized workers and staged violent labor movements in various cities of China, but failed. Mao Tse-tung, "the Native Communist," achieved greater success in leading the peasant movements. He, however, was not able to take control of the Chinese Communist Party until 1945 as will be seen in the following sections.

# The Life of Mao Tse-tung

*Before Becoming a Communist, 1893-1920*

Mao Tse-tung (1893-1976) was born on December 26, 1893, in the village of Shao Shan, Hsiang T'an county, Hunan province. His father, originally a poor peasant, had, through hard work, gradually moved up to become a rich peasant and grain merchant. At the age of about six, Mao began to work on the farm. Between the ages of eight and thirteen, he worked at farming tasks in the early morning and at night and attended a local primary school during the day to study the Chinese classics. In his spare time he enjoyed reading old Chinese novels, such as *The Tale of the Three Kingdoms* and *The Water Margin*. The strategy of war, rebelliousness, and heroism in them especially fascinated him.

At thirteen, he left the primary school and worked full-time on the farm in the day and kept books for his father at night. Disgusted with farming, he often quarreled with his father. When he was about fifteen, his father proposed to make him an apprentice in a rice shop but he insisted on attending the modern primary school where his cousin was a student. His father, opposed to this at first, was finally convinced by some friends that modern education would lead to better earning power. So at the age of sixteen Mao entered the school, where in a year's time he learned some foreign history and geography. He learned about Napoleon, Peter the Great, Catherine the Great, Gladstone, Wellington, Rousseau, Montesquieu, and Lincoln from a collection of biographies written in Chinese, known as *The Great Heroes of the World*.

At age seventeen, he entered a secondary school in Changsha, the capital of Hunan. Reading in a newspaper the revolutionary platform of Sun Yat-sen, he was greatly impressed. Shortly after the outbreak of the Revolution of October 10, 1911, he joined the revolutionary army of Li Yüan-hung, the Colonel who led the revolution against the Manchu regime. He left the army a few months later, when he learned that the civil war had been called off.

An advertisement for a higher commercial public school in

Changsha caught his attention. He registered there but could not follow most of the classes, as they were conducted in English and he knew scarcely more than the English alphabet.[1] One month later he joined another high school, but liked neither the curriculum nor the regulations and left in six months. He spent the next half year reading diligently by himself in the Hunan Provincial Library. He read Chinese translations of Adam Smith's *The Wealth of Nations,* Charles Darwin's *Origin of Species,* and works of J. S. Mill, Herbert Spencer, Montesquieu, and Rousseau. He also studied the history and geography of Russia, America, England, France, and other countries.

Although he considered his reading fruitful, he could not keep it up indefinitely. His family refused to support him unless he returned to school again. At this time he began to think seriously of making teaching his future career. He entered the Hunan Provincial First Normal School[2] in 1913 and was graduated in the spring of 1918.

During this period of his schooling he mastered the techniques of the classical essay and calligraphy and wrote many poems. He did not care to study English or any foreign language. Excellent in social science, he did poorly in natural science. He was opposed to the required courses in natural science and did not study them.[3] He was fascinated by *The New Youth,* the celebrated journal edited by Ch'en Tu-hsiu. He especially admired the articles written by the editor, and those by Hu Shih. During this period, he said, his mind was "a curious mixture of ideas of liberalism, democratic reformism, and utopian socialism."[4]

During the same period he was active socially and politically. He organized the student union of the First Normal School and helped found in Hunan the New People's Study Society for the study of modern thought. He participated in the organization of those Hunan students who planned to join the program of work and study in France that was sponsored by the Franco-Chinese Educational Association. In the summer of 1918 he accompanied some of these students to Peking, where they studied French before leaving for France.

He became an assistant of Li Ta-chao, Chief Librarian of National Peking University, in the fall of 1918. In the same year he joined the Marxist study group organized by Li. From late

1918 to mid-1920 he moved steadily toward Marxism. His faith in the doctrine of Marx, he said, was built up largely by reading translations of *The Communist Manifesto* by Marx and Engels, *Class Struggle* by Kautsky, and *History of Socialism* by Kirkup. By the summer of 1920 he considered himself a Marxist.[5]

### As a Communist, 1921-1949

Mao was one of the twelve delegates to the First Congress of the Chinese Communist Party, held secretly in Shanghai in the summer of 1921 under the direction of the Comintern agent Grigorii Voitinsky. At the Third Congress of the Party, which took place in Canton in June 1923, he was elected to the Central Committee. Since the policy of the Comintern called for the formation of a united front by the Chinese proletariat and peasantry with the Chinese bourgeoisie in order to seize power from the Kuomintang or Nationalist Party, the Congress officially approved the joining of the Kuomintang by individual Communists. In 1924 Mao became a reserve member of the Central Executive Committee of the Kuomintang, serving concurrently as the head of the Organization Bureau of the Central Committee of the Chinese Communist Party.

During the First Kuomintang-Communist United Front (1924-1927) for a national revolution against imperialism,[6] Mao participated as organizer of peasant associations in his native province of Hunan. He also trained organizers for the peasant movement in various other provinces. As he worked to motivate the peasants and promote their struggle against landlords, he recognized the enormous revolutionary potential of the peasantry. The peasants' revolutionary disposition was an effect of poverty, he believed, and that was why in his "Report on an Investigation of the Peasant Movement in Hunan" of March 1927[7], he recommended the use of poor peasants as the "vanguard of revolution" and intensification of the agrarian struggle for redistribution of land. His recommendation was rejected by the Central Committee of the Chinese Communist Party, then headed by Ch'en Tu-hsiu who believed in the orthodox Marxist teaching that the urban proletariat rather than the rural peasantry should be the "vanguard of revolution."

The termination of the First Kuomintang-Communist

United Front in the summer of 1927[8] was followed by a period of Communist resistance against Nationalist suppression. In October 1927, Mao led his peasant-worker army[9] in the Autumn Harvest Uprising in Hunan. The collapse of this uprising forced him to gather together the scattered units of his army and escape to a hideout in the Chingkangshan (Chingkang Mountains) on the Hunan-Kiangsi border. There he joined a group of bandits. Survivors of the Nanchang, Swatow, Canton, and other uprisings also came to this stronghold. In May 1928, he and Chu Teh combined what remained of their forces and built up the Fourth Red Army. Mao was its political commissar and Chu its commander.

It was at Chingkangshan that he developed the Red tactics of guerrilla warfare, whose essence was expressed in four slogans of the Red Army:

1. When the enemy advances, we retreat!
2. When the enemy halts and encamps, we trouble them!
3. When the enemy seeks to avoid a battle, we attack!
4. When the enemy retreats, we pursue![10]

Application of these tactics together with strict indoctrination in the basic ideology of Marx and Lenin made the small Red Army effective.

The failure of other uprisings in Central and Southern China caused more Red forces to escape to Chingkangshan in the winter of 1928. By January 1929 there was a shortage of food and clothing and the Nationalist troops had set up a blockade, so Mao and Chu at the head of the Red forces fought their way out of Chingkangshan into safer territory along the Kwangtung border. Finally, reaching Southern Kiangsi, they established their new base around Juichin. They instituted a Soviet Republic in Kiangsi province with Juichin as its capital in August 1929. In November 1931, Mao was made Chairman of the Chinese Soviet Republic.[11]

Chiang Kai-shek launched five major campaigns against the Soviet areas in Kiangsi between November 1930 and October 1933. The first four failed. The fifth succeeded in the encirclement of the Soviet areas. In early 1934, Juichin was seriously endangered. Over 100,000 soldiers of the Red Army and a number of civilian Communists were forced to evacuate Kiangsi and make the Long March northwestward.

The Long March, secretly planned, was completely on foot. Started in October 1934, it lasted about a year and covered some eight thousand miles. Its main columns were under the command of Mao and Lin Piao. The marchers followed difficult trails and crossed high mountain ranges and great rivers and gorges. They were frequently blocked or pursued by the Nationalist troops. In order to avoid occasional bombing and reconnaissance they marched as much as possible at night.

When the main columns of the Long March reached Tsunyi, Kweichou, in January 1935, Mao held a conference at which he attacked the returned students from Europe for their poor leadership in the Chinese Communist Party. It is generally believed that from then on he controlled the Chinese Communist Party.

Enduring much hardship, the marchers escaped to the northern border of Shensi province in October 1935. Only about 20 per cent or 20,000 soldiers of the Red Army remained.[12] They first established their headquarters in Paoan, Shensi. After occupying Yenan, Shensi, in December 1936, Mao made that city the new Red capital.

Following the kidnapping of Chiang Kai-shek in December 1936 at Sian, Shensi,[13] Mao sent Chou En-lai to Sian with the proposal that Chiang would be released on condition of making two promises: no further campaign against the Communists; and the formation of the Second Kuomintang-Communist United Front for the resistance of Japanese aggression. After making these promises, Chiang was released on December 25, 1936. From then on the Chinese Communists were able to expand in various parts of China.

Japanese troops occupied Peiping, the former name for Peking,[14] in July 1937. As they moved further south, they occupied the cities of North China and Central China and established puppet regimes with civil administration nominally in the hands of the Chinese. Large areas in the countryside were left with neither Japanese troops nor Japanese control of civil administration, so the Communists substituted themselves for the local authorities, indoctrinating the local population and expanding their armed forces. Meanwhile, the Japanese troops pushed further south. They captured Nanking, the Nationalist capital, in December 1937, and other major cities in the same year. In 1938 the Nationalist capital was moved to Chungking, Szechuan province.

In a long article entitled "The Chinese Revolution and the Chinese Communist Party" written in December 1939, Mao claimed that from 1927 to 1937 the upper stratum of the bourgeoisie, as represented by the reactionary bloc of the Nationalist Party, was in league with imperialism and formed a reactionary alliance with the landlord class. It turned against its friends, including the Chinese Communist Party, the proletariat, the peasantry, and the lower stratum of the bourgeoisie. For this reason Mao maintained that an armed struggle against the Nationalists was necessary. To ensure the success of the armed struggle other forms of struggle must also be employed. While the Red Army proceeded with its work in rural base areas, the Communist Party's propaganda and organization work must go on in the urban and rural areas controlled by the Nationalists. The Communist Party must have well-selected cadres working underground. Their tactic must be to advance slowly but surely, making the fullest possible use of all forms of open and legal activities permitted by laws, decrees, and social customs. The purpose of this was to accumulate Communist strength and bide time for the final seizure of power.[15] In other words, the strategy was to exploit the Second United Front to the fullest advantage, spending most of the Communist strength on military and political expansion rather than resistance against the Japanese.[16]

Under Mao's leadership, the Communists created their Shensi-Kansu-Ninghsia border government in March 1939. Later they established the Shansi-Hopeh-Chahar-Suiyüan border government. As they moved on to further expansion of their political and military power, clashes between the Communist and Nationalist forces occurred with increasing frequency.

In October 1939, when the western part of Shantung and Kiangsu were in danger of being under Communist control, the Nationalist government ordered the transfer of the Communist New Fourth Army stationed in that area to the north of the

Yellow river. It refused to obey. Instead, it expanded its operations in Kiangsu and in January 1941 had a major clash with Nationalist forces. The Nationalist government ordered it to disband and arrested its commander for court martial. Mao retaliated by authorizing the appointment of another commander and the expansion of the New Fourth Army.

Negotiations between the Kuomintang and the Communist Party took place in March 1943 and May 1944. Both broke down over Communist demands for further expansion of its army, for its army's legal status, for the recognition of the Communist-controlled areas as legitimate territory of the Communists, and for a constitutional coalition government.

By 1945 the Chinese Communist Party had nearly a million members and the Red Army reached a strength of equal number.[17] Mao and other leaders of the Communist border governments posed as democratic agrarian reformers. In their border governments only one-third of the offices were filled by actual Communists. The other two-thirds were equally divided between representatives of the peasants and those of the landlords. In this way, Mao created the impression that Chinese Communists differed from Russian Communists. After visiting the Communist capital of Yenan on November 7, 1944, General Patrick Hurley, President Roosevelt's special emissary in China, reported that ". . . the Communists (Chinese) are not in fact Communists; they are striving for democratic principles. . . ."[18]

The unconditional surrender of Japan on August 14, 1945, found Chiang Kai-shek's government totally unprepared. Mao Tse-tung, on the other hand, was ready for the harvest. A mad race took place between the Nationalist and Communist forces, each trying to reach the Japanese-occupied territories first in order to receive the Japanese surrender. The Communists enjoyed a distinct geographical advantage in this contest. They were in control of "liberated areas" in North, South, and Central China and their troops were deployed in the countryside of the Yellow, Yangtze, and Pearl river valleys. The Japanese-controlled major cities of Peiping, Tientsin, Shanghai, Nanking, Hankow, and Canton, which were located in these valleys, became islands in an ocean of Communists. Mao ordered a general offensive as early as August 9, 1945. Within two weeks of the Japanese surrender, the Communists expanded their territories from 116 to 175 counties,[19] a gain of 59 counties.

As the Nationalist forces, scattered along the several battle fronts and in West China, began to lose in the race with the Communist forces, the U.S. government lent its assistance to airlift some of the Nationalist units to the major cities and enable them to take them from the Japanese. Washington then ordered Tokyo to see to it that all Japanese forces in mainland China except in Manchuria,[20] on Taiwan, and in French Indochina north of the 16° parallel, be surrendered to Chiang Kai-shek and his representatives. The Nationalist government thus regained control of nearly all the important cities and communication centers in Central, East, and South China, while the Communist forces retreated temporarily to the countryside. The 59 counties which they had gained earlier, however, remained in their hands.

On August 28, 1945, Mao Tse-tung arrived in Chungking at the invitation of Chiang Kai-shek.[21] Six weeks of negotiations between the two Chinese leaders brought forth no settlement of such issues as the relative strength of the Nationalist and Communist forces, the integration of the two forces into a national army, the receiving of Japanese surrender, and the political control of "liberated areas."

The civil war that followed lasted until the fall of 1949. During this period, Mao never ceased to pave the road for his final seizure of power. In order to gain further support from the people, he adopted a policy of pacification. In an instruction to the Communist cadres written on November 7, 1945, he said

> See to it that in the liberated areas the peasants generally get the benefits of rent reduction and that the workers and other laboring people be benefited by appropriate wage increases and improved conditions; at the same time, see to it that the landlords can still make a living and that the industrial and commercial capitalists can still make profits. Unfold a large-scale production drive next year, increase the output of food and daily necessities, improve the people's livelihood. . . .[22]

Toward the end of 1945, fighting between the Nationalist and Communist forces became heavy. General George C. Marshall, special U.S. ambassador to China, arrived in China to mediate. His efforts led to a brief period of truce, but large-scale fighting again took place in April 1946. When the Russian troops finally withdrew from Manchuria in May 1946,[23] this territory was almost entirely under the control of the Chinese Communists. Marshall's further effort at mediation also failed.

By November 1948, Chiang Kai-shek's campaign to recover Manchuria proved to be a total failure,[24] despite the sacrifice of almost half a million of his best troops. The low morale of the Nationalist forces led to more victories for the Communists as they moved southward. In January 1949 they captured Tientsin and Peiping. In April and May 1949 respectively, they took over Nanking and Shanghai. As the conquest of all mainland China was in sight,[25] Mao Tse-tung, Chairman of the Chinese Communist Party, proclaimed on October 1, 1949, the establishment of the People's Republic of China with himself as its chairman. Peiping, now called Peking, was made the capital or seat of government.

## As Head of Both Party and State, 1949-1976

Mao's government, called the People's Democratic Dictatorship, was supposed to be the preliminary stage to the Marxist Dictatorship of the Proletariat. The idea for an intermediate form of government came to him almost ten years before the establishment of the People's Republic. In his article "On the New Democracy"[26] written in January 1940, he said that China, as a dependent country with feudal traditions, must practice "New Democracy" as the preliminary step to socialism. This policy called for the establishment of a democratic republic on the Leninist principle of democratic centralism. It would be under the joint dictatorship of all anti-feudal and anti-imperialist classes—the proletariat, the peasantry, the intelligentsia, and other sections of the petty bourgeoisie—headed by the proletariat. Its economic policy would be one of state ownership, but only of big banks and big industrial and commercial enterprises. The land of the landlord class would be confiscated and distributed to the poor peasants, but rich peasant economic activities would be tolerated. As to the duration of the period of the "New

Democracy," he did not specify. In another article "The Dictatorship of the People's Democracy,"[27] written in July 1949, he further confirmed the ideas he expressed in the earlier article and defined the Joint Dictatorship as a four-class bloc, consisting of the proletariat, the peasantry, the petty bourgeoisie, and the national bourgeoisie under the leadership of the proletariat.

From 1950 through 1952 Mao consolidated the state power through a number of major campaigns. One of them, the Movement for the Suppression of Counter-Revolutionaries, liquidated those who did not follow the Communist leadership, describing them as "reactionaries" or "enemies of the people."[28] The Three Anti and Five Anti Campaigns[29] constituted a "class war" against the bourgeoisie. As a result, members of the petty bourgeoisie and national bourgeoisie were largely removed from their positions. Some lost their lives; many ended up in prisons or labor camps for thought reform[30] and hard labor. In 1954, the government was reorganized and all non-Communists were eliminated from high government posts.[31] The less than five-year-old Joint Dictatorship was replaced by the Dictatorship of the Proletariat, comparable to that of the U.S.S.R.

The Movement for Agrarian Reform, another major campaign which was started in 1950, produced a violent peasant struggle against landlords. A great number of landlords were either killed or imprisoned or confined in labor camps. Land thus expropriated by the Government between 1950 and 1951 was subsequently distributed to about 70 per cent of the landless peasants. On January 1, 1953, the First Five-Year Plan (1953-1957) of China was launched. It was largely copied from the Soviet Five-Year Plan initiated by Stalin. Targets of production for the Five-Year Plan were established and material incentives were used to encourage production. To begin with, there was the formation of agricultural cooperatives in which cooperative peasants shared each other's tools and worked together on each other's land. The produce was divided into larger and smaller shares according to what each peasant put into the cooperative in the way of land, labor, and tools. In July 1955 Mao suddenly decided to convert the agricultural cooperatives into agricultural collectives, very much like the collective farms of the U.S.S.R. The government was to take over all land from private hands (without compensation) and call it "property of the state." Planning, management, supervision, and control of all land would become the business of the state. This decision was against the wishes of a majority of the Chinese Communist Party leaders and the advice of both Soviet and Chinese economic experts. Those who opposed it generally regarded the practice as premature. Collectives were large-scale enterprises. They required an industrial base that China had not yet achieved.[32] Mao, however, had deep faith in the inexhaustible productive potential of the Chinese peasants. He believed the peasants, when they were motivated through political indoctrination,[33] would have the will power to do wonders like the Foolish Old Man in the ancient Chinese fable who had mountains removed.[34] Were they not the well-indoctrinated Red forces which had won over the more numerous and much better-equipped Nationalist troops? Were they not the well-indoctrinated peasants who had liquidated the landlords? So long as the people were well indoctrinated, they would have determination enough for economic transformation. In 1956 all peasants were made to turn their land over to the collectives.[35] As all land belonged to the state, all peasants became wage-earners.

On the whole, the First Five-Year Plan was carried out with success. In the fall of 1957 Mao decided to outdistance the U.S.S.R. by moving China from socialism to communism, by effecting total rural and urban communalization. This was known as "the Great Leap Forward." Socialism, as it had been practiced in China, was founded on the Marxist idea of "to each according to his work." Quantity and quality of a person's work would decide what the wage would be. Under communism, also founded on Marxist theory, he would be recompensed on the principle "to each according to his need." His need would be determined by the Communist Party and Government. Private property would be completely abolished and people would live in communes.

Mao's commune was supposed to be the basic unit of the Communist society. It was not limited to the countryside. In addition to the agricultural communes that replaced the agricultural collectives, there were to be city communes and industrial communes. Each member of a commune, rural or urban, was supposed to turn everything he or she possessed over to the commune in return for food, clothing, shelter, medical care, and burial. Men and women would be forced to live separately. Children would be taken away from them and put under state care. When this system was put into practice, there was resistance, especially in the cities where people knew better how to ignore or short-circuit the Party cadres. Urban communalization practically stopped in 1958, although the drive for "backyard steel"[36] went on. In the meantime, the agricultural communes also met setbacks. Peasants who worked largely with primitive tools reached a point of physical exhaustion in their effort to attain impossible production targets. There was also passive resistance or "slow-down." Agricultural production lagged and not enough grains were produced to feed the people.

The failure of "the Great Leap Forward" led the Central Committee of the Communist Party, which was then under the control of Liu Shao-ch'i, first vice chairman of the Committee and future successor of Chairman Mao, and Teng Hsiao-p'ing, Party general secretary, to adopt two resolutions. One was to amend the commune system to be much like the former collective system; the other, to accept "Mao's request" to relinquish his concurrent post, chairmanship of the People's Republic of China, in order that he might have more time to pursue the theoretical works of Marx and Lenin.

When the Soviet-educated Liu Shao-ch'i succeeded as head of the State in 1959, he resumed the economic policy and methods used during the First Five-Year Plan. Material incentives were employed to promote agricultural and industrial production and greater emphasis was put on special knowledge and skill rather than on political indoctrination. The economy gradually got back on its feet. Mao, still insisting that politics should be in command of everything, including economics, criticized Liu as "the Chinese Khrushchev" who was practicing revisionism. "Redness" versus "expertise" thus became an acute ideological issue within the Party.[37]

Theoretically, the difference in ideology within the Party was not unexpected. In his article "On Contradiction"[38] Mao, summarizing the principles of contradiction as developed by Marx, Engels, Lenin, and Stalin, concluded by saying that there would be contradictions in society at all times, even after all class distinctions had been removed, even under communism. After the antagonistic contradictions between classes were removed, there would still be nonantagonistic contradiction within the socialist society. The nonantagonistic contradiction between the proletariat and the peasantry in socialist society could be resolved by the method of collectivization and mechanization in agriculture. The nonantagonistic contradiction within the Communist Party could be resolved by the method of criticism and self-criticism,[39] that is, the basic method of thought reform.

Liu, however, had the support of the majority of the members of the Party Central Committee and could not be subjected to thought reform. According to Mao, "if comrades who have committed mistakes can correct them, it will not develop into antagonism. . . . But if the people who have committed errors persist in them and aggravate them, there is the possibility that this contradiction will develop into antagonism."[40] Such antagonism could be resolved only through struggle, so the "Great Proletarian Cultural Revolution" of 1966 to 1969 was Mao's ideological and political struggle against Liu and Liu's faction in the Party. Since Liu had control over the Party organizations, including the Youth League, Mao was obliged to the "Red Guard"[41] as his own loyal fighting force. This body of young people, guided by the *Quotations from Chairman Mao Tse-tung*[42] (known as "the Little Red Book"), which expressed Mao's basic political thought, was directed by the Central Cultural Revolutionary Committee headed by Mao's private secretary, Ch'en Po-ta, and Mao's wife, Chiang Ch'ing. This committee, together with the Military Committee under Defense Minister Lin Piao, served as the center of command, but did not fully coordinate or cooperate. As different Maoist factions developed in the Red Guard and anti-Maoists infiltrated into it, fighting among them became increasingly vigorous. In the fall of 1968, the Maoists claimed to have seized control of all provinces, autonomous regions, and municipalities from their enemies, but bitter fighting kept on. In 1969, when Sino-Soviet border clashes in Manchuria and Sinking became both frequent and severe,[43] Mao decided to call off the nationwide small-scale civil war.[44] The Red Guard was suppressed by the army under

Lin Piao and millions of its members were sent to the country-side "to learn from the peasants"[45] by the order of Mao.

Mao's Cultural Revolution meant a great political victory for Mao. Liu was officially ousted from the Government in October 1968 and expelled from the Communist Party. Over one hundred government officials in high places were removed. In April 1969 when the Ninth Party Congress was held, about two-thirds of the members of the Central Committee of the Party were replaced by Mao's men. Mao was unanimously reelected Chairman of the Central Committee and Lin Piao was elected Vice Chairman of the Central Committee. Lin was also designated by Mao as his future successor.

The same congress adopted a new Party Constitution reaffirming "the Thought of Mao Tse-tung" as the guiding policy of both Party and State, but there was no going back to "the Great Leap Forward" policy. "To each according to his work" largely remained.

In 1973, about two years after his death in a plane crash, Lin Piao was formally accused of an unsuccessful attempt on Mao's life. The denunciation of Lin was followed by the Anti-Confucius Campaign, organized by Mao's wife Chiang Ch'ing and her faction. In this campaign, Confucius was accused of trying to bring back the old discarded system of slavery, and Lin Piao, the old discarded system of capitalism. All those who, like Confucius, tried to bring back discarded systems of any kind must be eliminated. The campaign aimed at purging Lin's former associates and other enemies of Chiang Ch'ing,[46] who were labelled as "capitalist roaders" or "revisionists." In February 1974 the *People's Daily* published the announcement that Chairman Mao would personally lead the anti-Confucius mass movement that he had initiated. This movement, however, did not get far or last long. Unlike the Cultural Revolution, there were no battles with real weapons; the battles were fought largely with wall posters and publications accusing certain named or un-named individuals or groups of moving toward "the capitalist road." By the end of 1974 the movement had subsided. Up to his death on September 9, 1976, Mao had not launched another major campaign.

## A Brief Analysis of Mao's Theory and Practice

Mao was a lifetime revolutionary in theory and practice. He was not an abstract thinker. His thought was developed in practice of the doctrines established by Marx, Engels, Lenin, and Stalin to whom he repeatedly acknowledged his indebtedness in his writings. In his major theoretical work "On Practice"[47] he says that no knowledge exists apart from practice. If one wishes to know the theory and methods of revolution, one must participate in revolution. Marxism-Leninism is the truth, because it has been verified in the practice of revolutionary class struggle and revolutionary national struggle. Discover the truth through practice, and through practice verify and develop the truth. Theory and practice are inseparable. Consequently, both doctrinairism and empiricism should be avoided.

He adopted and adapted Marxism-Leninism to the social and political conditions of China at different periods of time. In addition, he made use of Chinese traditions and concepts suitable for the realization of socialist ends. His early reading of Chinese history and novels on peasant uprisings, for instance, led him to believe in the Chinese saying "Poverty breeds rebellion." The Chinese peasantry was therefore in his view a traditional revolutionary force.[48] When he further realized that the Chinese proletariat was both small and weak, he made use of the peasantry instead of the proletariat as "the vanguard of revolution." When he proved to the world that it was in fact the peasantry that brought him revolutionary success, he drew the theoretical conclusion that in any dependent or underdeveloped country where the proletariat was small and weak, the peasantry could be indoctrinated and used as "the vanguard of revolution."

In the development of his guerrilla tactics Mao followed the precepts of *The Art of War* written by Sun Tzu, a well-known general who lived probably during the fourth century B.C. Victory with a minimum resort to force was the ideal. Primary emphasis was put on well-planned maneuvers, deceptive tactics, and espionage rather than head-on fighting against the enemy. That the troops must be well disciplined and their morale must be high, as advocated by Sun Tzu, was facilitated through indoctrination in Marxism-Leninism.

Mao believed in a flexible use of Leninist tactics and he used them effectively. His early practice of nonviolent land reform, of land reform without the liquidation of landlords, proved an effective tactic for advertising himself as an "agrarian reformer" and thus securing a great number of supporters. He made use of the petty bourgeoisie and national bourgeoisie during the First and Second Kuomintang-Communist United Front, and again during his "People's Democratic Dictatorship" in order to gain time to consolidate control. Without specifying the length of time in which he would practice the People's Democratic Dictatorship, he could replace it with the Dictatorship of the Proletariat as soon as he saw fit.

Like Lenin, he made use largely of political rather than military means to seize power. He used anti-Japanese propaganda to kidnap Chiang Kai-shek and win over a big following. He expanded his "liberated areas" by taking advantage of Japanese aggression. Much of his power was gained in an inexpensive way.

After he established the socialist regime, however, he made grave mistakes. He let politics take command of everything. He thought that anybody indoctrinated with his socialist thought would have the will to conquer hardship and that will power alone would be sufficient. His lack of knowledge of science and technology and of what was going on in the outside world[49] was probably the major factor which contributed to his blunders in "the Great Leap Forward."

The Cultural Revolution was a success insofar as the seizing of power from his enemies in the Communist Party was concerned; it was hardly an ideological victory. Liu and his faction were removed, but Liuism largely remained. The price paid for that revolution was high. It included the loss of many lives, a nationwide economic disruption, the closing of schools and colleges, and the sending of millions of students as well as the ex-student Red Guard to the countryside "to learn from the peasants." All this led to disastrous consequences. The loss and waste of brain power for national reconstruction, especially, would take a long time to restore.

Mao believed in "uninterrupted (perpetual) revolution," yet he did not launch another revolution comparable to the scope, intensity, or duration of the Cultural Revolution. Was this a matter of biding his time, which death prevented him from having, or did he finally realize that what was ideal in theory might not work well in practice?

## Notes

1. Edgar Snow, *Red Star Over China* (rev. and enlarged ed.) (New York: Grove Press, 1968), p. 143.

2. The nature and standing of a normal school in China was comparable to that of a teachers' college in the United States.

3. Snow, *Red Star Over China,* p. 145.

4. Ibid., pp. 148-49.

5. Ibid., p. 155.

6. For the First Kuomintang-Communist United Front, see Snow, pp. 114-15.

7. For this report, see Mao Tse-tung, *Selected Works of Mao Tse-tung* (later referred to as *Selected Works*), four vols. (Peking: Foreign Languages Press, 1967), vol. 2, pp. 23-59.

8. In the spring of 1927, the militancy of the peasant movement in Hunan, Hupeh, Kiangsi, and Fukien provinces alarmed the Kuomintang high officials and army commanders who demanded its suppression. The labor movement in various cities also became increasingly violent. As the Nationalist Government in Wuhan was dominated by the Soviet adviser Borodin and the Kuomintang left wing, the ministries of workers and peasants were headed by the Communists in the Kuomintang who had directed these movements. Consequently, Chiang Kai-shek ordered the purge of Communists from the Kuomintang. By the early summer of 1927 the Kuomintang-Communist United Front had been terminated.

9. His army, consisting largely of peasants, had a small number of miners in it.

10. Edgar Snow, *Red Star Over China,* p. 174.

11. In 1929, the First National Congress of the Chinese Soviet Republic convened at Juichin, Kiangsi. Delegates were representative of the major soviet areas in Kiangsi and other provinces, Red Army units, and the National General Labor Union. The National Congress authorized the establishment of a Provisional Central Soviet Government at Juichin and elected an executive committee which in turn elected Mao as its chairman. For details on the Soviet areas, see James P. Harrison, *The Long March to Power: A History of the Chinese Communist Party, 1921-72* (New York: Praeger, 1972), pp. 189-217.

12. For details on the Long March, see ibid., pp. 238-59 and Robert C. North, *Chinese Communism* (New York: McGraw-Hill, 1966), pp. 130-38.

13. On December 3, 1936, Chiang Kai-shek flew to Sian, Shensi, headquarters of Marshall Chang Hsüeh-liang who commanded the Manchurian troops. Chiang was there to discuss with Chang further plans and tactics

to use against the Communists. Unexpectedly on December 12, some of Chang's troops who had been persuaded by the Communists to fight against the Japanese rather than the Chinese Communists, mutinied and took Chiang as a captive.

14. In January 1929, when Chiang Kai-shek ended his Northern Expedition for the unification of China, Nanking (which literally means "Southern Capital") was made the capital of the Nationalist Government. The old capital Peking (which literally means "Northern Capital") was renamed Peiping or Northern Peace. When Mao Tse-tung established the People's Republic of China in October 1949, he made Peiping the capital, and restored the old name Peking.

15. For details, see "The Chinese Revolution and the Chinese Communist Party" in Mao Tse-tung, *Selected Works,* vol. 2, pp. 314-18.

16. During the period of the Second Kuomintang-Communist United Front, 1937-1945, the Red Army was entrenched in rural base areas behind the Japanese lines. As it seized more "liberated areas," it helped enforce moderate agrarian reform, such as reducing rents and interests of the poor peasants, instead of the violent peasant struggle against landlords. Similar moderate agrarian reform was adopted throughout the period of civil war, 1945-1949. This was to serve the purpose of preserving public order so that the Communists could concentrate all effort on destroying the Nationalist forces. A thorough discussion of this appears in "Tactical Problems of Rural Work in the New Liberated Areas," May 24, 1948, in Mao Tse-tung, *Selected Works,* vol. 4, p. 251. In the cities that were either controlled by the Nationalists or occupied by the Japanese but controlled by Chinese puppets, the Communist underground cadres infiltrated political, educational, religious, and social organizations and secretly directed their activities. Anti-imperialist propaganda did wonders in influencing the bourgeoisie. Sympathy for and support of the Communists were heightened, especially among intellectuals and students, many of whom were assimilated into the Chinese Communist organizations during the period of the Second United Front.

17. Jerome Ch'en, *Mao and the Chinese Revolution* (New York: Oxford University Press, 1967), p. 255.

18. Herbert Feis, *The China Tangle* (Princeton, New Jersey: Princeton University Press, 1953), p. 222.

19. Jerome Ch'en, *Mao and the Chinese Revolution,* p. 261.

20. Manchuria was an exception, because according to the Yalta agreement (agreed on by Stalin, Roosevelt, and Churchill) of February 1945, Soviet troops were to fight against the Japanese in Manchuria two to three months following the German surrender.

The Soviet troops actually moved to Manchuria to fight against the Japanese on August 8, 1945. They kept on with their advance despite the unconditional surrender of Japan six days later, and penetrated southward into the provinces of Jehol and Chahar in order to facilitate the entry of the Chinese Communist forces into Manchuria. They also turned over large quantities of surrendered Japanese arms to the Chinese Communists.

21. General Patrick Hurley, who tried to promote the unity of China, persuaded Mao to accept Chiang's invitation and vouched for the former's safety.

22. See "Rent Reduction and Production Are the Two Important Matters for the Defense of the Liberated areas," in Mao Tse-tung, *Selected Works*, vol. 4, p. 71.

23. Stalin's promise to Chiang Kai-shek that the Soviet troops would evacuate Manchuria within three weeks of Japan's defeat was not honored. For details, see Immanual C. Y. Hsü, *The Rise of Modern China* (2nd ed.) (New York: Oxford, 1975), pp. 734-35.

24. It proved that Chiang made a big mistake in rejecting the advice of General Albert C. Wedemeyer who believed that Chiang should consolidate the areas south of the Great Wall and north of the Yangtze and safeguard the communication lines in North China before trying to recover Manchuria.

25. Mao's conquest of mainland China was complete when the Nationalist government fled from Canton to Chungking on October 13 and to Taiwan on December 8, 1949.

26. "On the New Democracy" in Mao Tse-tung, *Selected Works*, vol. 2, pp. 339-84.

27. For "The Dictatorship of the People's Democracy," see ibid., vol. 4, pp. 418-19. For a thorough discussion of it, see Conrad Brandt, et al., *A Documentary History of Chinese Communism* (Cambridge, Mass.: Harvard University Press, 1952), pp. 456-58.

28. As recorded by Theodore H. White in an interview with Mao, "the people" referred to those who accepted the Chinese communist leadership and "the reactionaries," those who did not. "The reactionaries" were therefore "the enemies of the people." See Theodore H. White's documentary film: *China: Roots of Madness* (New York: West Glen Films, January 1967).

29. The Three Anti Campaign of 1951 was supposed to combat corruption, waste, and bureaucracy; and the Five Anti Campaign of 1952, to fight bribery, tax evasion, fraud, theft of government property, and leakage of state economic secrets.

30. Thought reform or "brainwashing" is a process of psychological coercion. It is based on Ivan Petrovich Pavlov's theory that environmental conditioning can change human will and human character. The basic method used in China is called "criticism" and "self-criticism," criticizing oneself and being criticized by one's group led by an activist for deviation from socialist ideology in thought and behavior from past to present. Fatigue from the heavy physical labor of the labor camp weakens an individual's will to resist. After a period of several months to a year of this daily bombardment combined with hard labor, most individuals experience an emotional crisis and submit themselves to the new faith. For details, see Robert J. Lifton, *Thought Reform and the Psychology of Totalism: A Study of "Brainwashing" in China* (New York: Vanguard Press, 1951).

31. Theodore H. E. Chen (ed.), *The Chinese Communist Regime: Documents and Commentary* (New York: Praeger, 1967), p. 60.

32. Nikita Khrushchev, who denounced Stalin in 1956 for the latter's abuse of power, was among those who thus criticized Mao's collective and later commune systems. His criticisms, together with his denunciation of Stalin, whom Mao greatly admired, led the Sino-Soviet relationship to turn from good to bad.

33. Political indoctrination, known as "Ideological Remolding" or "Socialist Indoctrination," was among the major campaigns carried on intensively from 1950 through 1952. It has never really stopped, though it varied in intensity from period to period.

34. In his speech at the Seventh National Congress of the Communist Party of China, June 11, 1945, Mao mentioned the ancient Chinese fable "The Foolish Old Man Who Removed the Mountains." The Foolish Old Man tried to dig up two huge mountains that obstructed the way to his house. He believed if he could not finish the job, his sons, or grandsons, or great-grandsons would. God was moved by his strong conviction and sent two angels to carry the mountains away. Mao said to the members of the Party that feudalism and imperialism were comparable to the two mountains to be dug up and the masses of the Chinese people took the place of God. When they worked under the leadership of the Communist Party, they could conquer every hardship. See Mao Tse-tung, *Selected Works*, vol. 3, pp. 271-72.

35. By 1956, the year of agricultural collectivization, Mao seemed to be confident that socialism in China was well established. Using the slogan "Let a hundred flowers bloom together; let a hundred schools of thought contend," he invited the intellectuals to criticize the government. The response was at first very cautious, but early in 1957 a bitter, outspoken attack was launched, especially by university students. Among other things, they complained of the Party domination of education and arts, its control of the press, and its corruption of justice. The Party struck back with a campaign against "rightists." Severe repression of the critics resulted, and the elimination or removal of the "counterrevolutionaries" or "enemies of the people" from their offices in both governmental and nongovernmental institutions. Universities were placed under surveillance and their students were forced to devote less time to study and more time to meetings for political indoctrination. Mao's speech "On the Correct Handling of Contradictions among the People" was published on June 10, 1957. This speech, popularly known to the people as "Let a Hundred Flowers Bloom," instructed the people that words and actions were right only when they in some way strengthened the socialist construction or Communist Party leadership. For this speech, see Stuart R. Schram, *The Political Thought of Mao Tse-tung* (rev. and enlarged ed.) (New York: Praeger, 1969), pp. 304-12; and Wm. Theodore de Bary, Wing-tsit Chan, and Chester Tan (comps.), *Sources of Chinese Tradition*, vol. 2 (New York: Columbia University Press, 1960), pp. 271-79. It is controversial as to whether Mao was genuinely surprised by the intensity of dissent expressed, or as suspected by many Chinese and foreign observers, including Nikita Khrushchev, that Mao might have called for open criticism to induce dissidents to reveal themselves so that he could identify them and wipe them out.

36. The people were instructed to melt down all house and household metal objects to produce steel in backyard furnaces. Steel thus produced in 1958 amounted to some three million tons. It was so inferior in quality, however, that it was unfit for industrial use as later disclosed. See Immanuel C. Y. Hsü, *The Rise of Modern China*, p. 789.

37. When Defense Minister P'eng Te-huai criticized Mao's "Great Leap Forward" and explained to Mao how important it was to create a modern professional army with up-to-date equipment, Mao argued that morale was more important than weapons and that political indoctrination was the way to elevate army morale. As a result of this difference in opinion, Mao dismissed P'eng and replaced him with Lin Piao as defense minister in 1959.

38. "On Contradiction," August 1937, in Mao Tse-tung, *Selected Works*, vol. 1, pp. 311-47. This article is generally regarded as one of the two major theoretical works of Mao. The other one is "On Practice," which will be discussed later.

39. See ibid., vol. 1, p. 322. For a brief explanation of "criticism" and "self-criticism," see Note 30.

40. See "On Contradiction" in Mao Tse-tung, *Selected Works*, vol. 1, p. 345.

41. The Red Guard was recruited from high school and college students. Between August 18 and November 26, 1966, Mao was reported to have reviewed in Peking 11,000,000 members of the Red Guard.

42. In 1967 alone, 350 million copies of *Quotations from Chairman Mao Tse-tung* as well as 86.4 million sets of Mao's *Selected Works* were printed. See Immanuel C. Y. Hsü, *The Rise of Modern China*, p. 860.

43. The Sino-Soviet dispute over the boundary line led to minor border clashes as early as 1963. Border negotiations in 1964 broke down. The conflict grew into major battles in 1968 and the situation turned worse in 1969.

44. Since the Red Guard was obsessed with the mission of eliminating "the Four Olds," old thought, old culture, old customs, and old habits, its members vowed to uphold the thought of Mao in order to make their country safe from bourgeois and revisionist influences. They ransacked private property, rampaged through the cities, and attacked anyone with modern attire, haircuts, or hairdos. They tortured Western-educated professionals, including professors, teachers, writers, artists, scientists, engineers, and medical doctors, as well as business men for their bourgeois thought. They pressured Liu Shao-ch'i and his wife into public "self-criticism" and demanded Liu's dismissal. They made victims of many other Party leaders, including Teng Hsiao-p'ing, Party general secretary, and Chu Teh, cofounder of the Red Army with Mao. As violent street fighting between the Maoists and anti-Maoists spread, bloodshed occurred in many parts of the country. It was truly a small-scale civil war.

45. Mao was reported to have said that he could not depend on the young intellectuals and students to carry on the revolution and that they should go to the countryside to learn from the peasants.

46. Premier Chou En-lai, who officially supported the Cultural Revolu-

tion but tried very hard to stop the Red Guard from going to excess, favored Teng Hsiao-p'ing. Following the Cultural Revolution, Chou set free Teng and a number of other Party leaders (including Chu Teh, but not Liu Shao-ch'i) who had been made victims of the Red Guard from house arrest or labor camps and rehabilitated them. He and the rehabilitated group became enemies of Chiang Ch'ing.

47. "On Practice," July 1937, in Mao Tse-tung, *Selected Works*, pp. 295-309.

48. His view might also have been influenced by his early Marxist mentor Li Ta-chao, who believed in the spontaneous revolutionary energies of the peasantry and the importance of the Communist revolutionary intelligentsia in providing it with leadership. See Maurice Meisner, "Li Ta'chao and the Intellectual Prerequisites for the Maoist Strategy of Revolution" in Chün-tu Hsüeh (ed.), *Revolutionary Leaders of Modern China* (New York: Oxford University Press, 1971), pp. 367-94.

49. See Note 3 for further comment on Mao's lack of knowledge of science and technology.

Mao had never traveled abroad until 1949 when he made his only trip to Moscow for the celebration of Stalin's seventieth birthday and to seek Russian aid and alliance. See Immanuel C. Y. Hsü, *The Rise of Modern China*, p. 809.

# 13

# Conclusion

$T$he mind of China has gone through two periods of development. During the first period—from ancient times to shortly before the middle of the nineteenth century—China secluded herself and developed her own systems of thought. Other than Buddhism, which was adopted and adapted from India, the prevalent schools of thought were almost entirely Chinese. In the second period—from shortly before the middle of the nineteenth century, when the impact of Europeans began to assume important dimensions,[1] to the present—the Chinese mind has been much influenced by the thought of the West. Sun Yat-sen's democracy was largely Anglo-American and Mao Tse-tung's socialism, predominantly Russian. Nevertheless, certain characteristics of the Chinese mind remain unchanged. Aspects of specifically Chinese thought have been preserved and even synthesized into borrowed foreign thought.

As observed by Professor Charles A. Moore, "For the Chinese, philosophy takes the place of religion—certainly for the educated and intellectual Chinese."[2] Philosophy is more important to the Chinese than to almost any other people in the world. A Chinese would sacrifice his life in defense of his philosophy as readily as a Christian martyr would defend his faith.[3] This is not to say that the Chinese as a people have never attached any importance to religion. Unlike a Western man who is often born into a religion and a philosophy of life that is a corollary of his religion, a Chinese of the presocialist days was governed by a Confucian code of ethics in his family and his social relations from the time of his birth. Whether or not he was to adopt a religion and what religion he should adopt would be his later concern.⁴ This made philosophy more than religion a foundation of his life and made social sanctions more influential than religious sanctions.⁵ After China became socialist, all religions were abolished by the government. Marxism-Leninism and the Thought of Mao Tse-tung took, or were expected to take, the place of both religion and philosophy in the life of the people.

Another characteristic of the mind of China is that the philosophy one adopts, or is made to adopt, must be practiced. In the old China, if one adopted the teachings of Confucius, one was expected to live by such teachings—not just to approve or admire them. In a similar way, socialist indoctrination of the people in the People's Republic of China aims at promoting not only an understanding of Marxism-Leninism and the Thought of Mao Tse-tung but the practice of these doctrines in words and action. Theory and practice must coincide. Philosophy and life are inseparable.

A third characteristc of the mind of China which has persisted from ancient times to the present is the greater emphasis on duties rather than on the rights of the people. There has not been a Chinese John Locke to define "life, liberty, and property" as natural rights with which men are born and government as the institution that preserves these rights. In the original teachings of Confucius, his regard for rights is implicit. His rules of conduct, or obligations incurred by the ruler and subject, the father and son, and by people in other human relations, emphasize the duties of each party according to his position. When both carried out their respective duties, both would enjoy their respective rights as results of the fulfillment of obligations on both sides. Confucius held that the man in a superior position was the more responsible. If a father did not act like a father, he could not expect his son to act like a son.⁶ Implicitly, Confucius meant that the son had the right to claim what was due him from his father. Mencius went as far as to justify rebellion against a bad ruler in terms not of the subject's demand for rights but of the ruler's failure to perform his duties, i.e., to ensure the subject's well-being.[7] The tradition of emphasizing duties rather than rights favors the more powerful party to a dispute, who is often able to demand performance of the duties of the other party rather than perform its own.

Despite the foreign influences of Buddhism, democracy, and socialism, certain aspects of Confucianism remained. Among the doctrines of the Chinese Buddhist School T'ien-t'ai (Lotus School), the "Mean" which was inspired by the mean of Confucius, was added to the Indian "Emptiness" and "Temporariness" to form the Threefold Truth.[8] Hu Shih condemned Confucianism as nondemocratic, yet he believed in and lived by Confucius' basic teaching that the individual must develop himself to the fullest in order to build a "paradise on earth" for the well-being of the people. Mao Tse-tung, who condemned Confucianism even more severely than Hu Shih, advocated such Confucian virtues as diligence and frugality,[9] modesty,[10] and discipline[11] for the advancement of socialism. He even quoted the phrases "to be insatiable in learning" and "to be tireless in teaching"[12] from *the Analects* (Book 7, chapter 33) as the best guide of the socialist. The content of "learning" and "teaching" has been changed, not the philosophy behind it.

It has been said that there is Taoism as well as Confucianism in every Chinese.[13] The basic Taoist concept of seeking harmony with nature rather than conquering and changing it has been suggested by both Hu Shih and Mao Tse-tung as the cause of the Chinese lack of adventurism and therefore of physical or material progress. Yet neither of them condemned Taoism as a whole. After going through the turmoil of "the Great Leap Forward" and "the Cultural Revolution," many Chinese drew consolation from the fact that they were better off than those who had been killed or "liquidated" and so they should be content. The Chinese, known as a people that can endure a great deal of hardship, depend on the Taoist concept of contentment to sustain them during bad times.

In the history of China before Mao Tse-tung, periods of a totalitarian system of government existed, but they were short. The long dynastic rules could be described on the whole as authoritarian, not totalitarian. As Professor Harold Vinacke points out, under dynastic rule there was "a highly centralized administrative system in a decentralized territorial system, the main feature of which was autocracy with some important democratic modifications."[14] The people were self-controlled through their own provincial and craft guilds, village council of elders, and family organizations. Their real life, both social and economic, was carried on without the direction of the officers of government. The First Emperor of Ch'in, who unified China, ruled for about eleven years (221-210 B.C.) by the practice of Legalism. After his death in 210 B.C., he and his Legalist advisers were severely condemned by the people. So there is good reason to believe that the people may deeply resent Mao's totalitarian system of government and his enforcement of socialism by Legalist methods. Organization of the "inhabitants' teams" and "inhabitants' committees" to cooperate with the government and to be responsible for each other's behavior[15] was a typical method of Legalist inspiration. China's traditional hatred of totalitarianism and her greater contact with the outside world following Mao's death may well be factors that will motivate change or modification of the government in both theory and practice.

The philosophical synthesis achieved during the Han period[16] suggests at least the possibility that China may have another period of the like activity—one in which compatible elements of the philosophies of East and West are integrated, and, through practical application of the new synthesis to government, produce a new system of politics. Such a system, if projected, would most likely assume a mean or middle position between the socialism of Russia and American democracy.

**Notes**

1. From this time on, the Westerners—first the Europeans and then also the Americans—succeeded in opening China for trade as the result of China's defeat in wars. For a brief account of the history of this period, see Kenneth Scott Latourette, *China* (Englewood Cliffs, New Jersey: Prentice-Hall, 1964), pp. 101-22.

2. Charles A. Moore (ed.), *The Chinese Mind: Essentials of Chinese Philosophy and Culture* (Honolulu, Hawaii: University of Hawaii Press, 1967), p. 1.

3. See pp. 51-52 on how the Confucian scholars sacrificed their lives because of their criticism of the government of Ch'in.

4. This was true of the majority of Chinese, including those whose

parents were Buddhists (as Buddhism has no sacrament such as baptism). The minorities whose parents were Christians or Moslems were, of course, exceptions. Even then they were not completely free from Confucian influence in society.

5. Probably for the same reason, the Chinese has little or hardly any prejudice against anybody's religion. It is the way a person behaves that matters, not his or her religion (which, to the Chinese, is essentially for the after life).

6. See p. 25 and Note 42 of Ch. 2.

7. See p. 43 and Note 9 of Ch. 5.

8. See pp. 67-68.

9. Mao Tse-tung, *Quotations from Chairman Mao Tse-tung* (New York: Bantam Books, 1967), pp. 105-09.

10. Ibid., p. 34.

11. Ibid., pp. 144-46.

12. Ibid., p. 178.

13. T'ung-chi Lin, "The Taoist in Every Chinese," *Tien Hsia Monthly,* 11 (Shanghai, 1940), 211-25.

14. Harold M. Vinacke, *A History of the Far East in Modern Times* (4th ed.) (New York: Appleton-Century-Crofts, 1941), p. 27.

15. See relevant documents in Theodore H.E. Chen (ed.), *The Chinese Communist Regime: Documents and Commentary* (New York: Praeger, 1967), pp. 109-13.

16. See Chapter 7.

# Bibliography

**General Works**

The following works are related to the subject matter of more than one chapter of this book.

Bodde, Derk. *Essays on Chinese Civilization*. Ed. and intro. by Charles Le Blanc and Dorothy Borei. Princeton, N.J.: Princeton University Press, 1981.

Brandt, Conrad. *Stalin's Failure in China*. New York: Norton, 1966.

Brandt, Conrad, Schwartz, Benjamin I., and Fairbank, John K. *A Documentary History of Chinese Communism*. Cambridge, Ma.: Harvard University Press, 1952.

Briere, O. S. J. *Fifty Years of Chinese Philosophy, 1898-1948*. Trans. from the French by Lawrence G. Thompson. New York: Praeger, 1965.

Chai, Winberg (ed.). *Essential Works of Chinese Communism: Mao Tse-tung, Liu Shao-ch'i, Lin Piao, P'eng Chen*. New York: Bantam Books, 1969.

Chan Wing-tsit (trans. and comp.). *A Source Book in Chinese Philosophy*. Princeton, N.J.: Princeton University Press, 1969.

Creel, Herrlee G. *Chinese Thought from Confucius to Mao Tse-tung*. New York: New American Library, 1960.

Dawson, Raymond (ed.). *The Legacy of China*. London and New York: Oxford University Press, 1964.

Day, Clarence Burton. *The Philosophers of China, Classical and Contemporary*. New York: The Philosophical Library, 1962.

de Bary, Wm. Theodore (and the Conference on Ming Thought). *Self and Society in Ming Thought*. New York: Columbia University Press, 1970.

de Bary, Wm. Theodore, Chan, Wing-tsit, and Watson, Burton (comps.). *Sources of Chinese Tradition*, vols. 1, 2. New York: Columbia University Press, 1964.

de Riencourt, Amaury. *The Soul of China: An Interpretation of Chinese History* (rev. ed.). New York: Harper and Row, 1965.

Eichhorn, Werner. *Chinese Civilization: An Introduction*. Trans. from the German by Janet Seligman. New York: Praeger, 1969.

Fairbank, John K. (ed.). *Chinese Thought and Institutions*. Chicago: Chicago University Press, 1957.

Fitzgerald, Charles P. *China: A Short Cultural History* (3rd ed.). London: Cresset, 1950.

Franke, Wolfgang. *China and the West: The Cultural Encounter, 13th to 20th Centuries.* Trans. from the German by R.A. Wilson. New York: Harper and Row, 1967.

Fung Yu-lan. *A History of Chinese Philosophy.* Two vols. Trans. by Derk Bodde. Princeton, N.J.: Princeton University Press, 1952 & 1953.

————. *A Short History of Chinese Philosophy.* Ed. by Derk Bodde. New York: Macmillan, 1948.

————. *The Spirit of Chinese Philosophy.* Trans. by E.R. Hughes. London: Kegan Paul, 1947.

Goodrich, L. Carrington. *A Short History of the Chinese People* (4th ed.) New York: Harper and Row, 1969.

Goodrich, L. Carrington and Fang Chaoying (eds.). *Dictionary of Ming Biography (1368-1644).* New York: Columbia University Press, 1976.

Harrison, John A. *China Since 1800.* New York: Harcourt Brace Jovanovich, 1967.

Houn, Franklin W. *A Short History of Chinese Communism.* Englewood Cliffs, N.J.: Prentice-Hall, 1967.

Hsiao Kung-chüan. *A History of Chinese Political Thought.* Trans. by Frederick W. Mote. Princeton, N.J.: Princeton University Press, 1979.

Hsieh Wu-liang. *Chung-kuo che-hsüeh shih* (A History of Chinese Philosophy). Taipei, Taiwan: Chung Hua Book Company, 1973.

Hsü, Immanuel C.Y. *The Rise of Modern China* (2nd. ed.). New York: Oxford University Press, 1975.

Hsüeh Chun-tu (ed.). *Revolutionary Leaders of Modern China.* New York: Oxford University Press, 1971.

Hu Shih. *Chung-kuo chung-ku ssu-hsiang shih ch'ang-pien* (A History of Medieval Chinese Thought). Taipei, Taiwan: Hu Shih Memorial Hall, Academia Sinica, 1973.

————. *Chung-kuo ku-tai che-hsüeh shih* (A History of Ancient Chinese Thought). Taipei, Taiwan: Commercial Press, 1958.

Hucker, Charles O. *China's Imperial Past: An Introduction to Chinese History and Culture.* Stanford, Ca.: Stanford University Press, 1975.

Hughes, Ernest Richard. *Chinese Philosophy in Classical Times* (rev. ed.). London: Dent, 1954.

Hummel, Arthur William (ed.). *Emminent Chinese of the Ch'ing Period (1644-1912).* Two vols. Washington, D.C.: U.S. Government Printing Office, 1943-44.

Latourette, Kenneth Scott. *The Chinese: Their History and Culture* (4th rev. ed.). New York: Macmillan, 1964.

Li, Dun J. (ed.). *The Essence of Chinese Civilization.* London: D. Van Nostrand, 1967.

Liang Ch'i-ch'ao. *Intellectual Trends of the Ch'ing Period.* Ed. and trans. by Immanuel C. Y. Hsü. Cambridge, Ma.: Harvard University Press, 1959.

Liu, Wu-chi. *A Short History of Confucian Philosophy.* New York: Dell, 1955.

Moore, Charles A. (ed.). *The Chinese Mind: Essentials of Chinese Philosophy and Culture.* Honolulu, Hawaii: East-West Center Press, 1967.

Moseley, George. *China Since 1911*. New York: Harper and Row, 1968.

Mote, Frederick W. *Intellectual Foundations of China*. New York: Knopf, 1971.

Nakamura, Hajime. *Ways of Thinking of Eastern Peoples: India-China-Tibet-Japan* (rev. English translation). Part 2 (on China). Honolulu, Hawaii: East-West Center Press, 1964.

Needham, Joseph. *Science and Civilization in China*, vol 2: *History of Scientific Thought*. Cambridge: Cambridge University Press, 1956.

North, Robert C. *Chinese Communism*. New York: McGraw-Hill, 1966.

——————. *Moscow and Chinese Communists* (2nd ed.). Stanford, Ca.: Stanford University Press, 1963.

Schwartz, Benjamin I. *Chinese Communism and the Rise of Mao*. Cambridge, Ma.: Harvard University Press, 1951.

Tan, Chester C. *Chinese Political Thought in the Twentieth Century*. Garden City, N.Y.: Doubleday, 1971.

Teng Ssu-yu and Fairbank, John K. *China's Response to the West: A Documentary Survey, 1839-1923*. New York: Atheneum, 1967.

Vinacke, Harold M. *A History of the Far East in Modern Times* (4th ed.). New York: Appleton-Century-Crofts, 1941.

Waley, Arthur. *Three Ways of Thought in Ancient China*. London: Allen and Unwin, 1939.

Wilbur, C. Martin and How, Julie. *Documents on Communism, Nationalism, and Soviet Advisers in China, 1918-1927*. New York: Columbia University Press, 1956.

Wright, Arthur F. (ed.). *Studies in Chinese Thought*. Chicago: University of Chicago Press, 1953.

**The Earliest Times**

Chang Kwang-chih. *Shang Civilization*. New Haven: Yale University Press, 1980.

——————. *The Archeology of Ancient China* (rev. ed.). New Haven: Yale University Press, 1968.

Creel, Herrlee G. *The Birth of China: A Survey of the Formative Period of Chinese Civilization*. New York: Ungar, 1937.

Karlgren, Bernhard (trans.). *The Book of Songs*. Stockholm: Museum of Far Eastern Antiquities, 1950.

Keightley, David N. *Sources of Shang History: The Oracle-Bone Inscriptions of Bronze Age China*. Berkeley: University of California Press, 1978.

——————. (ed.). *The Origins of Chinese Civilization*. Berkeley: University of California Press, 1982.

Legge, James (trans.). *The Ch'un T'sew* (Spring and Autumn Annals) with *The Tso Chuen* ("The Chinese Classics," vol. 5). London: Oxford University Press, 1872 and later editions.

——————. *The I Ching* (Book of Changes). Ed., intro. and study guide by Ch'u Chai with Winberg Chai. New Hyde Park, N.Y.: University Books, 1964.

——————. *The Li Ki* (Book of Rites) (Sacred Books of the East, vols. 27 and

28). London: Oxford University Press, 1926. (Both *Ta Hsüeh* [Great Learning] and *Chung Yung* [Doctrine of the Mean] are contained in *The Li Ki.)*

——. *The She King* (Book of Poetry) ("The Chinese Classics," vol. 4). London: Oxford University Press, 1871 and later editions.

——. *The Shoo King* (Book of Historical Documents) ("The Chinese Classics," vol 3). London: Oxford University Press, 1865 and later editions.

Li Chi. *The Beginnings of Chinese Civilization: Three Lectures Illustrated with Finds at Anyang.* Seattle, Washington: University of Washington Press, 1957.

MacHovec, Frank J. (trans.). *I Ching* (The Book of Changes). Mount Vernon, N.Y.: Peter Pauper Press, 1971.

Waley, Arthur (trans.). *The Book of Songs.* London: Allen and Unwin, 1937.

Watson, William, *Early Civilization in China.* New York: McGraw-Hill, 1966.

Wilhelm, Helmut. *Change: Eight Lectures on the I Ching.* Trans. from the German by Cary F. Baynes. New York: Harper and Row, 1960.

**Confucius**

Cheng T'ien-hsi. *China Moulded by Confucius: The Chinese Way in Western Light.* London: Stevens and Sons, 1946.

Creel, Herrlee G. *Confucius and the Chinese Way.* New York: Harper and Row, 1960.

Legge, James (trans.). *The Confucian Analects* ("The Chinese Classics," vol. 1). London: Oxford University Press, 1893 and later editions.

Lin Yutang (ed.). *The Wisdom of Confucius.* New York: Random House, 1938.

Pound, Ezra (trans.). *Confucius: The Great Digest, The Unwobbling Pivot, The Analects.* New York: New Directions, 1969.

Waley, Arthur (trans.). *The Analects of Confucius.* London: Allen and Unwin, 1938.

Ware, James R. (trans.). *The Sayings of Confucius.* New York: New American Library, 1955.

**Mo Tzu**

Mei Yi Pao. *Motse, the Neglected Rival of Confucius.* London: Probsthain, 1934.

——. (trans.). *The Ethical and Political Works of Motse.* London: Probsthain, 1929.

Mo Tzu. Harvard-Yenching Institute Sinological Index Series, Supp. 21, 1948; reprinted 1961.

Watson, Burton (trans.). *Mo Tzu: Basic Writings.* New York: Columbia University Press, 1963.

**The Taoists: Lao Tzu and Chuang Tzu**

Blakney, Raymond B. (trans.). *The Way of Life: Lao Tzu.* New York: New American Library, 1955.

Chan Wing-tsit. *The Way of Lao Tzu, a Translation and Study of the Tao-te Ching.* New York: Bobbs-Merrill, 1963.

Cheng Lin (trans.). *The Works of Lao Tzyy: Truth and Nature.* Taipei, Taiwan: World Book, 1969.

Creel, Herrlee G. *What Is Taoism? And Other Studies in Chinese Cultural History.* Chicago: University of Chicago Press, 1970.

Duyvendak, J. J. L. (trans.). *Tao te ching, the Book of the Way and Its Virtue.* London: J. Murray, 1954.

Giles, Herbert A. (trans.). *Chuang Tzu, Taoist Philosopher and Chinese Mystic.* London: Allen and Unwin, 1961.

Grahm, A. C. (trans.). *Chuang Tzu: The Inner Chapters.* Winchester, Ma.: Allen and Unwin, 1982.

Kaltenmark, Max. *Lao Tzu and Taoism.* Trans. from the French by Roger Greaves. Stanford, Ca.: Stanford University Press, 1969.

Legge, James (trans.). *The Tao Teh King* (Sacred Books of the East, vol. 39). London: Oxford University Press, 1891.

——————. *The Writings of Kwang-tze* (Chuang Tzu). (Sacred Books of the East, vol. 39). London: Oxford University Press, 1891.

Lin Yutang (trans. and ed.). *The Wisdom of Laotse.* New York: Random House, 1948.

Merton, Thomas. *The Way of Chuang Tzu.* New York: New Directions, 1965.

Waley, Arthur. *The Way and Its Power; a Study of the Tao te ching and Its Place in Chinese Thought.* New York: Grove Press, 1958.

Ware, James R. (trans.). *The Sayings of Chuang Tzu.* Text in both English and Chinese. Taipei, Taiwan: Confucius Publishing, 1970.

Watson, Burton (trans.). *Chuang Tzu: Basic Writings.* New York: Columbia University Press, 1964.

——————. *The Complete Works of Chuang Tzu.* New York: Columbia University Press, 1968.

Welch, Holmes, *Taoism: The Parting of the Way* (rev. ed.). Boston: Beacon Press, 1965.

Wu, John C. H. (trans.). *Tao teh ching.* New York: St. John's University Press, 1961.

## Prominent Followers of Confucius: Mencius and Hsün Tzu

Dubs, Homer H. *Hsüntze: The Moulder of Ancient Confucianism.* London: Probsthain, 1927.

——————. (trans.). *The Works of Hsüntze.* London: Probsthain, 1928.

Hsün Tzu. Harvard-Yenching Institute Sinological Index Series, Supp. 22, 1950.

Legge, James (trans.). *The Works of Mencius.* (The Chinese Classics, vol. 2). London: Oxford University Press, 1895.

Richards, I. A. *Mencius on the Mind.* London: Kegan Paul, 1932.

Ware, James R. (trans.). *The Sayings of Mencius.* New York: New American Library, 1960.

Watson, Burton, *Hsün Tzu: Basic Writings*. New York: Columbia University Press, 1963.

## The Legalists: Shang Yang, Han Fei, and Li Ssu

Bodde, Derk. *China's First Unifier, a Study of the Ch'in Dynasty as Seen in the Life of Li Ssu*. Leiden: E.J. Brill, 1938.

Chen En-cheng. "Han Fei's Principle of Government by Law," *Chinese Culture*, 1:4 (1958) 91-103.

Duyvendak, J. J. L. (trans.). *The Book of Lord Shang*. London: Probsthain, 1928.

Liao Wen-kuei (trans.). *The Complete Works of Han Fei-tzu*. Two vols. London: Probsthain, 1939 and 1960.

Watson, Burton (trans.). *Han Fei Tzu: Basic Writings*. New York: Columbia University Press, 1964.

## Philosophical Synthesis of the Han

Tung Chung-shu. *Ch-un Ch'iu Fan Lu. Su Pu Ts'ung K'an* edition.

Yao Shan-yu. "The Cosmological and Anthropological Philosophy of Tung Chung-shu," *Journal of the North China Branch of the Royal Asiatic Society*, 73 (Shanghai, 1948) 40-68.

## Neo-Taoism and Buddhism

Chan Wing-tsit. *Religious Trends in Modern China*. New York: Columbia University Press, 1953.

———. "Transformation of Buddhism in China," *Philosophy East and West*, 7 (1957-58) 107-16.

Chang, Chen-chi. *The Buddhist Teaching of Totality; the Philosophy of Hua Yen Buddhism*. University Park, Pa.: Pennsylvania State University Press, 1971.

———. *The Practice of Zen*. New York: Harper and Row, 1959.

Ch'en, Kenneth K.S. *Buddhism in China, a Historical Survey*. Princeton, N.J.: Princeton University Press, 1964.

———. *The Chinese Transformation of Buddhism*. Princeton, N.J.: Princeton University Press, 1973.

———. "Neo-Taoism and the Prajna School during the Wei and Chin Dynasties," *Chinese Culture*, 1:2 (1957) 33-46.

Conze, Edward. *A Short History of Buddhism*. Winchester, Ma.: Allen and Unwin, 1982.

———. *Buddhism; Its Essence and Development*. New York: Harper and Row, 1959.

———. *Buddhist Meditation*. London: Allen and Unwin, 1956.

Fung Yu-lan (trans.). *Chuang Tzu, a New Selected Translation with an Exposition of the Philosophy of Kuo Hsiang*. Shanghai: Commercial Press, 1933.

Hu Shih. "Ch'an (Zen) Buddhism in China: Its History and Method," *Philosophy East and West*, 3 (1953) 3-24.

Lau, Dim Cheuk (trans.) *Tao Te Ching* (the Wang Pi version). Baltimore: Penguin Books, 1971.

Ogata, Sohaku. *Zen for the West.* London: Rider, 1959.

Petrov, A. A. *Wang Pi, His Place in the History of Chinese Philosophy.* Institute of Oriental Studies Monograph 13. Moscow Academy of Science, 1936.

Suzuki, Daisetz Teitaro. *Essays in Zen Buddhism.* First Series, London: Luzac, 1927; Second Series, 1933; Third Series, 1934.

————. *Manual of Zen Buddhism.* New York: Grove, 1960.

————. *Studies in Zen.* New York: Philosophical Library, 1955.

————. *The Zen Doctrine of No-Mind.* London: Rider, 1949.

————. "Zen: A Reply to Hu Shih," *Philosophy East and West,* 3 (1953) 25-46.

Takakusu, Junjro. *The Essentials of Buddhist Philosophy.* Ed. by Wing-tsit Chan and Charles A. Moore. Honolulu: University of Hawaii Press, 1947.

T'ang Yung-t'ung. "Wang Pi's New Interpretations of the I Ching and Lun-yü." (Walter Liebenthal trans.). *Harvard Journal of Asiatic Studies,* 10 (1947) 75-88.

Thomas, Edward J. *The History of Buddhist Thought.* London: Kegan Paul, 1933.

Von Heinrich, Dumoulin. *The Development of Chinese Zen after the Sixth Patriarch in the Light of Mumonkan.* Trans. from the German by Ruth Fuller Sasaki. New York: First Zen Institute of America, 1953.

Watts, Allan W. *The Spirit of Zen: A Way of Life, Work and Art in the Far East.* (3rd ed.). New York: Grove Press, 1958.

————. *The Way of Zen.* New York: Vintage Books, 1957.

Welbon, Guy Richard. *The Buddhist Nirvana and Its Western Interpreters.* Chicago: University of Chicago Press, 1968.

Zücher, E. *The Buddhist Conquest of China.* Two vols. Leiden: Brill, 1959.

## Neo-Confucianism and the Reaction against Neo-Confucianism

Bruce, J. Percy. *Chu Hsi and His Masters: An Introduction to Chu Hsi and the Sung School of Chinese Philosophy.* London: Probsthain, 1923.

————. *The Philosophy of Human Nature by Chu Hsi.* London: Probsthain, 1922.

Chai Ch'u. "Neo-Confucianism of the Sung-Ming Periods," *Social Research* 18 (1951) 370-92.

Chang, Wing-tsit. "How Buddhistic Is Wang Yang-ming?" *Philosophy East and West* 12 (1962) 203-16.

————. (trans.). *Introduction for Practical Living and Other Neo-Confucian Writings.* New York: Columbia University Press, 1963.

Chang, Carsun. *The Development of Neo-Confucian Thought.* Two vols. New York: Bookman Associates, 1957.

————. *Wang Yang-ming, the Idealist Philosopher of Sixteenth-Century China.* New York: St. John's University Press, 1962.

Chiang Fan (1761-1831). *Kuo-ch'ao Han-hsüeh shih-ch'eng chi* (Biographies of

Leaders of the Han Learning of the Present Dynasty). Published by Juan Yüan, 1818.

*Erh-Ch'eng ch'üan-shu* (Complete Works of the Two Ch'engs). Pao-Kao-t'ang (ed.). K'ang-hsi period (1662-1722).

Freeman, Mansfield. "The Philosophy of Tai Tung-yüan," *Journal of the North China Branch of the Royal Asiatic Society,* 64 (Shanghai, 1933) 50-71.

Fung Yu-lan. "The Philosophy of Chu Hsi," trans. by Derk Bodde from *Chung-Kuo Che-hsüeh shih* (vol. 2, 896-927). *Harvard Journal of Asiatic Studies* 7 (Cambridge, 1942) 1-51.

Henke, Frederick Goodrich (trans.). *The Philosophy of Wang Yang-ming.* Chicago and London: Open Court, 1916.

Hu Shih. *Tai Tung-yüan ti che-hsüeh* (The Philosophy of Tai Tung-yüan). Shanghai: Commercial Press, 1927.

Huang Siu-chi. *Lu Hsiang-shan, a Twelfth Century Chinese Idealist Philosopher.* New Haven: American Oriental Society, 1944.

Tai Chen. *Meng Tzu tsu-i shu-cheng* (Commentary on the Meanings of Terms in the Book of Mencius). Chengtu, 1924.

T'ang Chu-i. "Chang Tsai's Theory of Mind and Its Metaphysical Basis," *Philosophy East and West* 6 (1956) 113-36.

Ts'ai Yung-ch'un (trans. and ed.). *The Philosophy of Ch'eng I, a Selection of Texts from the "Complete Works."* Typescript. New York: Columbia University, 1950.

## Sun Yat-sen

Amann, Gustav. *The Legacy of Sun Yat-sen; a History of the Chinese Revolution.* Trans. from the German by Frederick Philip Grove. New York: L. Carrier, 1929.

Bruce, Robert. *Sun Yat-sen.* London: Oxford University Press, 1969.

Hsü, Leonard S.L. *Sun Yat-sen: His Political and Social Ideals.* Los Angeles: University of Southern California Press, 1933.

Linebarger, Paul Myron Anthony. *The Political Doctrines of Sun Yat-sen; An Exposition of the San min chu i.* Baltimore: Johns Hopkins Press, 1937.

————. *Sun Yat-sen and the Chinese Republic.* New York: AMS Press, 1969.

Martin, Bernard. *Strange Vigour; a Biography of Sun Yat-sen.* Port Washington, N.Y.: Kennikat Press, 1970.

Schiffrin, Harold Z. *Sun Yat-sen and the Origins of the Chinese Revolution.* Berkeley: University of California Press, 1968.

————. *Sun Yat-sen, Reluctant Revolutionary.* Boston: Little, Brown, 1980.

Sharman, Abbie Mary. *Sun Yat-sen, His Life and Its Meaning; a Critical Biography.* New York: John Day, 1934.

Sun Yat-sen. *Kuo-fu chüan-shu* (Complete Works of the Founding Father). Taipei, Taiwan: Kuo-fang Research Institute, 1960.

————. *Memoirs of a Chinese Revolutionary; a Programme of National Reconstruction for China.* New York: AMS Press, 1970.

—————. *San Min Chu I* (Three Principles of the People). Trans. by Frank W. Price. Shanghai: Commercial Press, 1928.

Wilbur, Clarence Martin. *Sun Yat-sen, Frustrated Patriot*. New York: Columbia University Press, 1976.

## Leading Proponents of a New Culture: Ch'en Tu-hsiu and Hu Shih

Ch'en Tu-hsiu. *Tu-hsin wen-ts'un* (Collected Essays of Ch'en Tu-hsiu). Four volumes. Shanghai: Ya-tung Bookstore, 1927.

Chih Yü-ju. "Ch'en Tu-hsiu: His Career and Political Ideas," *Revolutionary Leaders of Modern China*. Ed. by Hsüeh Chun-tu.

—————. *The Political Thought of Ch'en Tu-hsiu*. Ph.D. diss., Indiana University, 1965.

Chou Tse-tung. *The May Fourth Movement: Intellectual Revolution in Modern China*. Stanford, Ca.: Stanford University Press, 1967.

Grieder, Jerome B. *Hu Shih and the Chinese Renaissance*. Cambridge, Ma.: Harvard University Press, 1970.

How, Julia Lien-ying. *The Development of Ch'en Tu-hsiu's Thought, 1915-1938*. M.A. Thesis, Columbia University, 1949.

*Hsian-tao chou-pao* (The Guide Weekly) (main organ of the Chinese Communist Party) (reprint). Five vols. Tokyo: Daian, 1963.

*Hsin ch'ing-nien* (The New Youth) (reprint). Fourteen vols. Tokyo: Daian, 1962.

Hu Shih. "Dr. Hu Shih's Personal Reminiscences," Interviews compiled by Te-kong Tong, with Dr. Hu's corrections in his own handwriting, 1958. Typescript in the archives of the Oral History Project, Columbia University.

—————. *Hu Shih liu-hsüeh jih-chi* (Hu Shih's Diary while Studying Abroad), four vols. Taipei, Taiwan: Commercial Press, 1959.

—————. *Hu Shih wen-ts'un* (Collected Essays of Hu Shih, Coll. 1-4). Four vols. Taipei, Taiwan: Far East Book Co., 1953.

—————. *Ssu-shih tzu-shu* (A Self-Account at Forty). Taipei, Taiwan: The Far East Book Co., 1959.

—————. *The Chinese Renaissance* (2nd ed.). New York: Paragon Book Reprint, 1963.

*Hu Shih ssu-hsiang p'i-p'an* (A Critique of Hu Shih's Thought). Eight vols. Peking: San-lien Bookstore, 1955.

Meisner, Maurice. *Li Ta-chao and the Origins of Chinese Marxism*. Cambridge, Ma.: Harvard University Press, 1967.

Shih, Vincent. "A Talk with Hu Shih," *China Quarterly* 10 (April-June 1962) 149-65.

Yang Ch'eng-pin. *Hu Shih che-hsüeh ssu-hsiang* (The Philosophical Thought of Hu Shih). Taipei, Taiwan: Commercial Press, 1966.

—————. *Hu Shih ti cheng-chih ssu-hsiang* (Hu Shih's Political Thought). Taipei, Taiwan: Commercial Press, 1967.

## Mao Tse-tung

Barnett, A. Doak. *Communist China and Asia*. New York: Vintage Books, 1960.

Bennett, Gorden and Montaperto, Ronald N. *Red Guard*. Garden City, N.Y.: Doubleday, 1972.

Boorman, Scott A. *The Protracted Game: a Wei-ch'i Interpretation of Maoist Revolutionary Strategy*. New York: Oxford University Press, 1969.

Bouc, Alain. *Mao Tse-tung: A Guide to His Thought*. Trans. from the French by Paul Auster and Lydia Davis. New York: St. Martin's Press, 1977.

Chambre, Henri. *From Karl Marx to Mao Tse-tung, a Systematic Survey of Marxism-Leninism*. Trans. from the French by Robert J. Olsen. New York: Kennedy, 1963.

Chen, Theodore H.E. (ed.). *The Chinese Communist Regime: Documents and Commentary*. New York: Praeger, 1967.

—————. *Thought Reform of the Chinese Intellectuals*. London: Hong Kong University Press and Oxford University Press, 1960.

Ch'en, Jerome. *Mao*. Englewood Cliffs, N.J.: Prentice-Hall, 1969.

—————. *Mao and the Chinese Revolution*. London and N.Y.: Oxford University Press, 1965.

—————. (ed.). *Mao Papers, Anthology and Bibliography*. London and New York: Oxford University Press, 1970.

Chesneaux, Jean. *China: The People's Republic, 1949-1976*. Trans. from the French by Paul Auster and Lydia Davis. New York: Pantheon Books, 1979.

Cohen, Arthur A. *The Communism of Mao Tse-tung*. Chicago: University of Chicago Press, 1964.

Compton, Boyd. *Mao's China: Party Reform Documents, 1942-1944*. Seattle, Washington: University of Washington Press, 1952.

Esmein, Jean. *The Chinese Cultural Revolution*. Trans. from the French by W.J.F. Jenner. Garden City, N.Y.: Doubleday, 1973.

Feis, Herbert. *The China Tangle*. New York: Atheneum, 1965.

FitzGerald, Charles Patrick. *Mao Tse-tung and China*. New York: Holmes and Meier, 1976.

Floyd, David. *Mao against Khrushchev; a Short History of the Sino-Soviet Conflict*. New York: Praeger, 1964.

Gittings, John. *Survey of the Sino-Soviet Dispute*. London and New York: Oxford University Press, 1968.

Goodstadt, Leo. *China's Search for Plenty, the Economics of Mao Tse-tung*. New York: Weatherhill, 1973.

Harrison, James Pinckney. *The Long March to Power: A History of the Chinese Communist Party, 1921-72*. New York: Praeger, 1972.

Hawkins, John N. *Mao Tse-tung and Education: His Thoughts and Teachings*. Hamden, Ct.: Linnet Books, 1974.

Hsiao Yü. *Mao Tse-tung and I Were Beggars*. Syracuse, N.Y.: Syracuse University Press, 1959.

Karnow, Stanley. *Mao and China; from Revolution to Revolution.* New York: Viking Press, 1972.

Keesing's Research Report. *The Cultural Revolution of China.* New York: Charles Scribner Sons, 1967.

Leys, Simon. *Chinese Shadows.* New York: Penguin, 1978.

Lifton, Robert J. *Revolutionary Immortality: Mao Tse-tung and Cultural Revolution.* New York: Random House, 1968.

──────. *Thought Reform and the Psychology of Totalism: A Study of "Brainwashing" in China.* New York: Random House, 1951.

MacFarquhar, Roderick (ed.). *China Under Mao: Politics Takes Command.* Cambridge, Ma.: The MIT Press, 1966.

Mao Tse-tung. *On Guerrilla Warfare.* Trans. and with an intro. by Samuel B. Griffith. New York: Praeger, 1961.

──────. *Quotations from Chairman Mao Tse-tung.* Ed. with an intro. and notes by Stuart R. Schram. New York: Praeger, 1967.

──────. *Selected Military Writings* (2nd ed.). Peking: Foreign Languages Press, 1967.

──────. *Selected Works of Mao Tse-tung.* Four vols. Peking: Foreign Languages Press, 1965-67.

Mu Fu-sheng. *The Wilting of the Hundred Flowers: The Chinese Intelligentsia under Mao.* New York: Praeger, 1963.

Payne, Pierre Stephen Robert. *Mao Tse-tung.* New York: Weybright and Talley, 1969.

Rice, Edward E. *Mao's Way.* Berkeley: University of California Press, 1972.

Schram, Stuart R. *Mao Tse-tung.* New York: Simon and Schuster, 1966.

──────. *The Political Thought of Mao Tse-tung* (rev. and enl. ed.) New York: Praeger, 1969.

Schwartz, Benjamin I. *Communist China: Ideology in Flux.* Cambridge, Ma.: Harvard University Press, 1968.

Shu, Austin C. *On Mao Tse-tung; a Biographic Guide.* East Lansing, Mich.: Asian Studies Center, Michigan State University, 1972.

Snow, Edgar. *Red Star Over China* (rev. and enl. ed.). New York: Grove, 1968.

Solomon, Richard H. *Mao's Revolution and the Chinese Political Culture.* Berkeley: University of California Press, 1971.

Terrill, Ross. *Mao: A Biography.* New York: Harper and Row, 1980.

Uhalley, Stephen, Jr. *Mao Tse-tung: A Critical Biography.* New York: New Viewpoints, 1975.

Wilson, Dick. *Anatomy of China: An Introduction to One Quarter of Mankind.* New York: The New American Library, 1969.

──────. (ed.). *Mao Tse-tung in the Scales of History: A Preliminary Assessment Organized by the China Quarterly.* Cambridge: Cambridge University Press, 1977.

Zagoria, Donald S. *The Sino-Soviet Conflict, 1956-61.* New York: Atheneum, 1966.

# Index

*Analects of Confucius,* 20-21, 22, 23, 73
Anti-Confucius campaign, 118
*Art of War, The,* 119

Bodhidharma, 68-69
*Book of Changes,* 20
*Book of History,* 20
*Book of Lord Shang, The,* 48
*Book of Music,* 20
*Book of Poetry,* 14, 20
*Book of Rites,* 20, 73
Borodin, Mikhail, 86
Buddha, 63-64
Buddhism, 38, 61, 63-70

Cantlie, James, 83
Ch'an (Meditation) school, 67, 68-70
Ch'an (Zen), 38
Chan Tsai, 73
Chang Hsün, 85
Chao Kao, 52
Ch'en Chiung-ming, 86
Ch'en Po-ta, 117
Ch'en Tu-hsiu, 86, 94-96, 104, 107
Ch'eng, 51
Cheng Hao, 75
Cheng Yi, 73
Chiang Ch'ing, 117, 118
Chiang Kai-shek, 91, 99, 100, 108, 109, 111, 112, 113
Chih-k'ai (Chih'i), 67
"Chinese Revolution and the Chinese Communist Party, The," 110

*Ch'ing-nien tse-chih* (The Youth Magazine), 94
Chou dynasty, 12, 13, 18
Chou En-lai, 109
Chou Tun-yi, 73
Ch'ü Ch'iu-pai, 104
Chuang Tzu, 35, 63
*Chuang Tzu, The,* 35, 37-39, 62
Chu-Hsi, 73, 75
Chu Teh, 108
*Ch'un-ch'iu fan-lu,* 55, 58
*Class Struggle,* 107
*Commentary on the Book of Changes,* 62
*Commentary on the Book of Waterways,* 101
*Commentary on the Chuang Tzu,* 62, 63
*Commentary on the Lao Tzu,* 62
*Communist Manifesto,* 107
Confucianism, 22-26, 32-33, 42, 44-45, 47, 54, 72-73, 94-95, 100, 129
Confucius, 12, 18-26, 62
*Criticisms of the Thought of Hu Shih,* 101
Cultural Revolution, 117-18, 120

Darwin, Charles, 96-97, 106
*Descent to the Island of Lanka,* 68-69
Dewey, John, 96, 98, 100
"Dictatorship of the People's Democracy, The," 114

Earlier Han, 54

Early Chou, 12, 14, 18, 52
Engel, Friedrich, 107

Fabian Society, 90
Fa-shun, 68
Fa-tsang, 68
First Five-Year Plan, 114-15, 116
Flower Garland Scripture, 68
*Four Books, The,* 73
Fu-hsi, 11

George, Henry, 84, 90
Great Leap Forward, 115-16
*Great Heroes of the World, The,* 105
*Great Learning, The,* 75

Han Confucianism, 54-59
Han dynasty, 26, 45
Han Fei, 49-50
*Han Fei Tzu, The,* 49
Han Kao-tsu (Liu Chi), 54, 56
Hinayana, 66, 67
*History of Socialism,* 107
Hsia dynasty, 11-12, 13
*Hsin ch'ing-nien* (The New Youth),
 94, 95, 106
Hsun-Tzu, 33, 44-45, 49
*Hsün Tzu, The,* 41
Hu Shih, 96-102
Huang Hsing, 84
Huang-ti (Yellow Emperor), 11
Hua-yen (Flower Garland) school,
 67, 68
Hui-k'e, 69
Hui-neng, 69
Hurley, Patrick, 111
Huxley, Thomas, 98

*Instructions for Practical Living,* 76

James, William, 96
Joffe, Adolph, 86, 88

Kautsky, Karl, 107
*Kidnapped in London,* 84
Ku Yen-wu, 78
Kuo Hsiang, 61, 62

Lao Tzu, 35, 62
*Lao Tzu, The,* 35, 37, 38, 39, 61, 62
Late Chou, 12, 52
Later Han dynasty, 63
Legalism, 47-52
Li Li-san, 104
Li Ssu, 49, 50-52
Li Tao-chao, 46, 95, 106
Li Yüan-hung, 85, 105
Lin Piao, 117
Lincoln, Abraham, 88
Liu Chi (Liu Pang), 54
Liu Shao-ch'i, 116
Long March, 109
*Lotus of the Wonderful Law,* 67
Lu Hsiang-shan, 75
Lun Yü, 20-21

Mahayana Buddhism, 66
Manchu (Ch'ing) dynasty, 77, 81
Mao Tse-tung, 104-21, 129
Marshall, George C., 112-13
Marx, Karl, 84, 90, 95, 107
*Mean, The,* 75
Mencius, 41-44
*Mencius, The,* 41, 73
*Meng Tzu tsu-i shu-cheng,* 78
Middle Chou, 12, 18
Mill, John Stuart, 84, 106
Ming dynasty, 75
Mo Tzu, 29-33
Moism, 30-33
Montesquieu, 84, 88, 106

Neo-Confucianism, 38, 72-78
Neo-Taoism, 61-63
New Culture Movement, 94, 95,
 101

"On Contradiction," 116-17
"On Practice," 119
"On the New Democracy," 113
*Origin of Species,* 106
*Outline of the History of Chinese
 Philosophy,* 101

*Progress and Poverty,* 90

*Quotations from Chairman Mao Tse-tung,* 117

Red Guard, 117-18, 120
"Report on the Investigation of the Peasant Movement in Hunan," 107
Revolution of 1911, 82, 85
Rousseau, Jean-Jacques, 106
Russo-Japanese War, 84

School of Han Learning, 77-78
School of the Mind, 75-77
Second (Summer) Revolution, 85
Shang dynasty, 12, 13
Shang Yang, 48
Shen-hui, 69
Shen-nung, 11
Shun, 11, 23
Siddhartha Gautama, *see* Buddha
Sino-Japanese War, 81
Smith, Adam, 106
Sneevliet, J. F. M. (*pseud.* H. Maring), 86
Spencer, Herbert, 106
*Spring and Autumn Annals,* 20
Sui dynasty, 63, 72
Sui-jen, 11
Sun Tzu, 119
Sun Yat-sen, 82-91

Sung dynasty, 45, 72, 75

Tai Chen, 78
*Tale of the Three Kingdoms, The,* 105
T'ang, 12, 13
T'ang dynasty, 45, 63, 72
Taoism, 35-39, 129
Teng Hsiao-p'ing, 116
Theravada Buddhism, 66
T'ien-t'ai (Lotus) school, 67-68
Tung Chung-shu, 55-56
Tzu Ssu, 42

Voitinsky, Grigorii, 95, 107

Wang Pi, 62
Wang Yang-ming, 75-77
*Water Margin, The,* 105
*Wealth of Nations, The,* 106
Wen, 12, 13
Wildcat Ch'an school, 77
Wu, 12, 13, 23, 54, 55

Yao, 11
Yen Hui, 62
Yen Yüan, 78
Yü, 11-12
Yüan dynasty, 75
Yüan Shih-k'ai, 85
Yu-ch'ao, 11

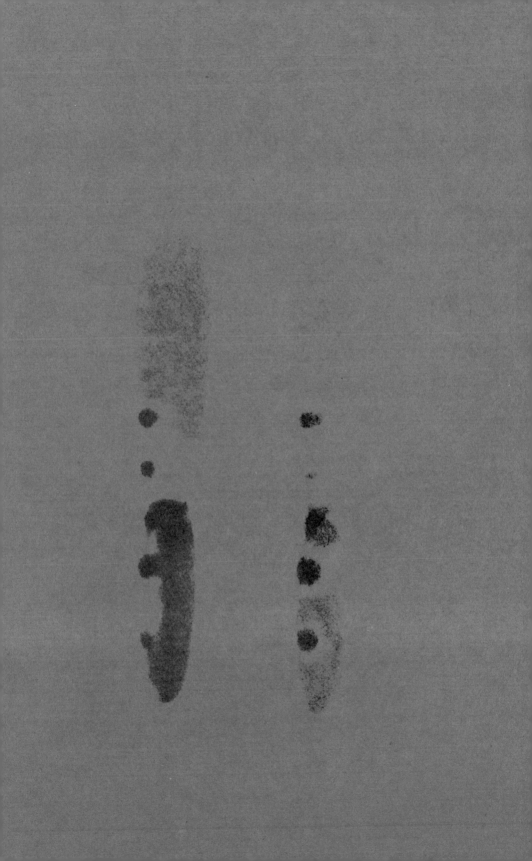